Living
CONTACT

THE
SECRET
OF THE
OVERCOMING
LIFE

JESUS IS LORD

KENNETH
COPELAND
PUBLICATIONS

Living Contact
The Secret of the Overcoming Life

ISBN 1-57562-149-5   30-0533

07 06 05 04 03 02   7 6 5 4 3 2

© 1997 Gloria Copeland

Kenneth Copeland Publications
Fort Worth, Texas 76192-0001

For more information about Kenneth Copeland Ministries, call 1-800-600-7395 or visit www.kcm.org.

Table of Contents

Preface

We are in the last of the last days. It's time to move into a closeness with God where you live separated unto Him and obey Him in all the things in your life. Jesus said, "If you abide in Me and My Words abide in you, ask what you will and it will be done" (see John 15:7). That's living contact. And it has great reward.

Living contact with God means spending time with Him. It's a lifestyle of talking to Him, listening to Him and obeying what you hear and what you find in the written Word. Learning to live in the place where God can talk to you at any moment *is* the secret to living the overcoming life.

Staying in living contact with Him is, without question, the number one priority of the Christian life. It is the key that opens every spiritual door.

Living contact makes faith work. It's the way love works. Living contact with God produces the anointing that enables us to lay hold of all the wonderful things God has provided for us through Jesus Christ.

Preface

If we aren't in living contact with God, it doesn't really matter how much we know. We can be full of information about faith. We can understand how it comes, what it does and how to release it. We can study about love until we have memorized every love scripture in the Bible. We can know the steps to healing and prosperity backward and forward. But we won't have the *power* to put those things into action unless we spend time with God and maintain a living connection with Him.

What you will have in your life tomorrow will be determined by what is in your heart today. So when you fill your heart with the Word and the voice of God, if you make living contact with Him each day and feast your heart on His promises and His presence, your future will be one of joy and prosperity, healing and health. Instead of chasing after the blessings of God, you'll find they're chasing you and overtaking you at every turn! Understanding this message changed my life forever.

Gloria Copeland

1

First Things First

During my years of walking with the Lord, He has taught me many wonderful things. He has taught me about faith and righteousness, healing and prosperity. He has taught me so many vital truths from His Word for which I am so grateful. And He's teaching me more every day.

Yet, even so, if you were to ask me to name the most important principle of Christian living that I've learned, I could answer you without hesitation.

It is the secret of maintaining a living connection with God.

Staying in living contact with Him is, without question, the number one priority of the Christian life. It is the key that opens every spiritual door.

Living contact makes faith work. It's the way love works. Living contact with God provides the power that enables us to lay hold of all the wonderful things God has provided for us through Jesus Christ.

If we aren't in living contact with God, it doesn't really matter how much we know. We can be full of information about faith. We can understand how it comes, what it does and how to release it. We can study about love until we have memorized every love scripture in the Bible. We can know the steps to healing and prosperity backward and forward. But we won't have the *power* to put those things into action unless we spend time with God and maintain a living connection with Him.

When all is said and done, it's not what we know that counts, it's what we do. And without vital, continual union with God, we won't be spiritually strong enough to do what we know to do!

It's amazing how many Christians don't realize that. They rush around trying to do things in their own strength. They run from one good thing to the next trying to serve the Lord. But because they don't maintain a living connection with God, they end up tired, frustrated and defeated.

They're like Martha was on the day that Jesus ministered in her house. Instead of sitting down at Jesus' feet and listening to Him teach the Word like her sister, Mary, the Bible says:

Martha (overoccupied and too busy) was distracted about much serving; and she came up to Him and said, Lord, is it nothing to You that my sister has left me to serve alone? Tell her then to help me—to lend a hand and do her part along with me. But the Lord replied to her by saying, Martha, Martha, you are anxious and troubled about many things; There is need of...only one. Mary has chosen the good portion—that which is to advantage—which shall not be taken away from her (Luke 10:40-42, *The Amplified Bible*).

An Awesome Privilege

As you can see from Mary's example, there is nothing complicated about establishing a living connection with Jesus. Even the newest believer can do it. Making living contact with God is simply fellowshiping with Him. It's talking to Him and listening to Him. It's setting aside the distractions and demands of life and taking the time to commune with Him in His Word and in prayer.

Some people say, "Well, I'd like to do that, but my schedule just won't permit it."

Actually, I don't believe they would say that if they realized what an awesome privilege it is to fellowship with Almighty God. If they had a genuine revelation of the fact that the Creator and Ruler of the entire universe has made Himself available to meet personally with them every day, they would change their schedule. They would find some way to make time for Him.

Think about what an amazing opportunity it is to personally commune with God. Adam and Eve had that opportunity in the Garden of Eden. God would come and walk with them in the cool of the day.

But then they sinned and lost their ability to have that kind of contact with God. They died spiritually, so they were unable to respond to Him as they once did. Instead of standing righteous and unashamed in His presence, when He came calling for them, they had to run and hide because they were full of shame and condemnation.

What a loss! What a tragedy that was!

For 4,000 years afterward, mankind was locked out of the presence of God by sin. Even the Israelites, God's special people, were unable to fellowship freely with Him. When they needed divine help or healing, they had to go to the priest. And though the priest had the anointing of God upon him, even he couldn't go boldly into God's presence whenever he wanted. Only the high priest could go behind the thick veil of the temple into the holy of holies where the presence of God dwelt. And he could only go there once a year with great precaution, and always with the blood of an animal, to atone for his sin as well as the people's.

But, hallelujah, when Jesus went to the cross for us, all that changed! He paid the price for our sins. He shed His own blood to not just atone for sin but to remit it. His sacrifice of Himself for us restored man's lost fellowship with God.

Now as born-again believers, we *"have full freedom and confidence to enter into the [Holy of] Holies [by the power and virtue] in the blood of Jesus"* (Hebrews 10:19, *The Amplified Bible)*. God is accessible to us once again. He has made us new creations and put His own Spirit inside us so that we ourselves can be temples of the living God. He has given us His righteousness so that instead of hiding from the presence of God, we can *"come boldly unto the throne of grace, that we may obtain mercy, and find grace to help in time of need"* (Hebrews 4:16).

God's consecrated people for thousands of years longed to experience what we have today. They yearned to be able to come directly into God's presence. They wanted to be able to commune with Him any time of the day or night as we can.

My, what a privileged people we are!

God has thrown open to us the door of fellowship. He has said, "I'm here for you. Just draw near to Me and I'll draw near to you. I'll give you the wisdom you need. I'll strengthen you and equip you and help you in every area of your life."

Yet how many Christians are daily taking advantage of that wonderful privilege?

Too few. They're too busy with the affairs of life to take the time for it.

"Well, Gloria," you might say, "considering how much we have to do these days, that's understandable."

Is it? Think about it from another perspective for a moment, and I think you'll change your mind.

Suppose you woke up one morning, walked into your kitchen and Jesus was sitting at the table. "Well, *Jesus!*" you said with surprise. "I'm thrilled You came by. I've really been wanting to see You. I have some problems I need Your help with...I wish I had time to talk to You about them right now, but I have to run. I'm having lunch downtown and I have to take care of some business. Maybe we'll have time to talk a while when I come home tonight."

Then, when you arrived home you had a Little League game, so you rushed out the door saying, "I'm sorry, Jesus. I have to go to the game right now. But we'll spend a few minutes together before I go to bed tonight, OK?"

The problem was, when you returned from the Little League game, you were so tired you thought, *I just need to watch a little television to relax.* Then you ended up falling asleep in front of the television, while Jesus continued to sit and wait for you at your kitchen table. Finally, the day slipped completely away, and you missed your opportunity to be with Him.

Of course, you probably think you would never do such a thing. If Jesus physically came to your house, you'd stop everything just to be with Him. Yet, when you understand how real the spirit realm is, when you fully realize that His precious Holy Spirit is right there inside you, waiting for you day after day, you'll see that it's just as foolish to neglect your daily fellowship with Him in the Word and in prayer as it would be to leave Jesus sitting alone at your kitchen table.

It is my prayer that as you read this book, the Holy Spirit will give you a deeper revelation of that truth. That He will strengthen you in your commitment to put first things first and make a living contact with Jesus every day.

I know from experience, it will forever change your life.

2

A Lifestyle of Living Contact

Of course, even after you make Jesus the Lord of your life, it takes more than a few casual contacts with God to learn how to be an overcomer. It takes a lifestyle of living contact with Him. If we truly want to see what God can do, we can't be content to run to Him only in the hard times, when we're in desperate need. We can't be satisfied to work Him into our schedule when it's convenient. We must build our schedule around our time with Him. We must seek God in prayer and the Word every single day, when things are hard and when they're easy, in good times and in bad.

If you think about it, that's just plain smart.

After all, God is the One Who has all the answers. He knows where you need to go in life and how to get you there. He has the solution for every problem.

But He won't run you down to get your attention so He can give you those solutions. No, He will wait for you to do your part. What is your part? To draw near to Him. If you'll do that, He'll draw near to you in return. He gave us His Word on it (James 4:8). Hebrews 10:22 says, *"Let us draw near with a true heart in full assurance of faith...."*

When you call on God, you will never be answered by "voice mail." You'll never hear a recording like you do so often when you make phone calls these days. You'll never hear Him say, "Hello, this is God. I'm away from the throne right now. Please leave a message and I'll return your call as soon as I can."

No, He is always there for us. So if you feel like He hasn't been talking to you lately, you had better check up on yourself and see how much you've been talking to Him. If you don't feel like He's been paying enough attention to you, then start paying more attention to Him!

The moment you turn to Him, He'll be there for you.

As I said before, however, don't wait until hard times come to turn to Him. Develop a lifestyle of living contact. Fellowship with the Lord daily when things are going well so that when trouble comes, you'll be spiritually strong enough to overcome.

Jesus said in the world we will have tribulation (John 16:33). It doesn't matter who you are or how rich or well-educated, or even how much faith you have, in this life you will face some tests and trials. The devil is roaming around this Earth seeking to kill, steal and destroy—and you will have to deal with him. So you'd better get ready. Jesus, our Champion and Savior, also said, *"I have overcome the world."* When we stay in vital union with Him, we can get victory in the time of trouble.

You may not be in a desperate situation today, but as long as you live on this Earth, you will need your faith. This is a crazy world, and this is a critical hour. If you want to survive in it successfully, you'll have to latch onto the power of God.

This is not the time to be a lukewarm, lazy Christian. This is the time to be on fire for God, because nothing else will work. The closer we approach the end of this age, the less dependable natural things will be. In the days ahead, there will be more diseases that medicine can't cure. There will be financial problems and social problems that men can't solve.

In times like these (or in any other times, actually), there is just one sure source of supply and that's God. And only by letting Him be God in our lives, by making Him number one and by putting time with Him ahead of ourselves, our families, our careers and everything else, will we be able to walk through these troubled times in triumph.

It would surprise some people to hear me say that. They think faith preachers teach that you won't have any problems if you live by faith. But if that's what they think, they obviously have never listened to Ken or me, because we don't say you won't have any problems. We just say that when the problems come, you'll have an answer for them.

Everyone in the world has trouble, sinners and saints alike. The difference is that when a Bible-believing, Spirit-filled child of God faces trouble, he doesn't face it alone. God says, *"I will be with him in trouble; I will deliver him, and honour him"* (Psalm 91:15).

Who is with you in trouble makes a big difference. If your only help is your own natural strength and resources, you might come out of that trouble all right...and you might not. But if God is with you, you can be sure you'll come through just fine!

The Victory Is in Your Heart

That's why it's important to develop a lifestyle of living contact with God. That's why it's important to make the time you spend with Him in prayer and in the Word your priority during the good times. You want to be sure that in the hard places you'll be so accustomed to looking to Him, you won't let the feelings or circumstances of the moment pull you away from that attitude of dependency. You want to be strong in your communion with God, so that you have the assurance and the power to cast down the fears and imaginations and threats of the devil that come during times of trouble.

You also want to daily develop your ability to hear from Him so that when you're in a desperate place, you'll know how to listen for His voice.

Just one word from God can change your whole situation in a moment. Ken and I have experienced that again and again through the years. We've been in times of deep trouble. We've faced situations that looked impossible. But God always helped us and brought us through in victory.

On one particular occasion, we fell behind on our television bills and found ourselves almost $6 million in the red. (That might not seem like much money to you, but to us it was serious! We aren't used to owing anybody anything. Everything in our ministry, including all our buildings, is debt free.) With every day that passed, those television bills kept rolling in, and we just kept falling further behind. Month after month went by with no improvement. Naturally speaking, we made every adjustment we knew to make. Yet nothing seemed to help.

So Ken and I just kept walking by faith, making contact with God day after day in prayer and in the Word. There were times when even *that* didn't appear to be making any difference. But we live by faith and not by sight, so when we would become tired and want to faint, we would just pick ourselves up and feed our faith with God's Word. We would get back to that place of faith where He could sustain us by His strength and power.

Then one day, something happened inside of us. The Spirit of God moved in our hearts and we received the breakthrough. Aggressive faith took hold and despite the fact that the bills were still unpaid, we knew in our hearts the money we needed was ours.

Sure enough, within just a few months, that impossible-looking debt was paid!

Once we had the victory on the inside, the circumstances had to bow their knee, because victory on the inside always brings victory on the outside. That's a spiritual fact. Once you lay hold of deliverance, healing or prosperity in your heart, all the devils in hell can't stop it from coming to pass in your life.

That's why daily living contact with God is absolutely vital to your success—because victory is won first in the heart, then in the circumstances.

3

Abiding in the Vine

In the 15th chapter of John, Jesus reveals to us just how important abiding in Him truly is. He considered it such a crucial matter that He spoke to His disciples strongly about it just before He went to the Cross. Therefore, we should pay especially serious attention to the Words He said.

You may have read them many times before, but take a moment and read them again carefully as if you were reading them for the first time.

I am the true vine, and my Father is the husbandman. Every branch in me that beareth not fruit he taketh away: and every branch that beareth fruit, he purgeth it, that it may bring forth more fruit. Now ye are clean through the word which I have spoken unto you.

Abide in me, and I in you. As the branch cannot bear fruit of itself, except it abide in the vine; no more can ye, except ye abide in me. I am the vine, ye are the branches: He that abideth in me, and I in him, the same bringeth forth much fruit: for without me ye can do nothing.

If a man abide not in me, he is cast forth as a branch, and is withered; and men gather them, and cast them into the fire, and they are burned. If ye abide in me, and my words abide in you, ye shall ask what ye will, and it shall be done unto you. Herein is my Father glorified, that ye bear much fruit... (John 15:1-8).

To understand what Jesus was saying there, you must realize that He is not just instructing us to enjoy occasional times of fellowship with Him. He is telling us to abide in Him. The word *abide* has a sense of permanency about it. It doesn't mean to come in and go out. It refers to the place where you remain and dwell continually.

When Ken and I travel, we might stay in a hotel for a week. We live there temporarily, but we don't abide there. We abide at our house in Fort Worth. That's where all our belongings are. That's where we continually live.

By the same token, when Jesus said *"Abide in me,"* He wasn't saying "Live in fellowship with Me one day and with the world the next." He wasn't talking about a sporadic or temporary arrangement. He was instructing us to make that place of dependency and communion with Him our permanent home.

And He immediately told us why we must do that. It's because if we don't, we won't be able to produce any fruit in our lives. If we're not continually walking with Him and talking with Him, continually spending time in His Word and listening for the Spirit's direction on the inside, spiritually we won't be able to accomplish anything!

Contrary to what many people seem to think, you cannot live from Sunday to Sunday, fellowshiping with the Lord just once a week at church and ignoring Him the rest of the time, and still live a reasonably successful Christian life. Jesus was quite clear about that. Read again what He said in John 15:6: *"If a man abide not in me, he is cast forth as a branch, and is withered; and men gather them, and cast them into the fire, and they are burned."*

The moment a branch is broken off from the vine, it begins to die. It doesn't matter how close they are to one another. You can lay that branch right up next to the vine, but if the union has been broken, there will be no life flow. There will be no sap flowing from the vine into the branch.

The same is true for us. When we become too busy to spend time with God in prayer and in His Word, when we become preoccupied with natural, earthly things and disconnect from communion with Him, we immediately begin to wither.

The word *wither* means to *shrivel, to lose or cause to lose energy, force or freshness.* That's a vivid picture of what happens to us when we aren't in vital contact and living union with the Lord. We still belong to Him. We still have His life within us, but His energy is not flowing through us, so we can't produce anything.

We lose our capacity for spiritual action. We may know what to do, but we find ourselves lacking the power to do it. We lose our desire to do the work God has called us to do. And even those things we are able to do become dry and spiritless.

Have you ever been to a church and heard an old, dead sermon? When you walked out of that service you might have said, "My goodness, that was dry!" The reason it was dry was that it didn't flow from a heart that had made living contact with God.

I'm not saying the preacher was in deep sin or terribly backslidden. On the contrary, he may have spent years fellowshiping with God. But you can't store up that living connection. It's like the manna the children of Israel ate in the wilderness. It must be fresh every day.

I don't care how great an orator you may be, you can't preach a good sermon if you aren't living in union and communion with the Lord. People try all the time. They'll work hard to come up with eloquent phrases and great ideas. They might even buy a book and preach a sermon that was written by an anointed man or woman of God. But that sermon won't be as good when a dried up preacher preaches it, because if he hasn't been making living contact with God, there won't be any life behind his words.

Of course, preachers aren't the only ones who dry up when they don't maintain living contact with God. Anyone who fails to abide in Jesus will be spiritually barren. Jesus made that very plain. He didn't stutter. He just said straight out that unless we abide in Him we *"can do nothing."*

I'm not sure very many Christians believe that. If they did, they wouldn't be so prone to skip their time with God.

If they really believed John 15:5, instead of thinking, *I'm too busy to take time to pray and read the Word today,* they'd think, *My schedule is so packed, I'd better get up early so I can spend some extra time with God! I can't afford to be a spiritual* do-nothing *today. I need to produce a lot of fruit!*

We all need to adopt that kind of attitude. We need to acknowledge that we can't do anything on our own. But we shouldn't be stuck there. We shouldn't just go around talking about how helpless we are without Jesus. That's not productive. What we need to do is say, "Without Him I can do nothing BUT, PRAISE GOD, I'M NOT WITHOUT HIM! I'M WITH HIM, AND I CAN DO ALL THINGS THROUGH HIM WHO STRENGTHENS ME!"

We need to make up our minds to abide in Him and then just center on the fact that when we abide in Him, He abides with us and enables us to bear much fruit.

Power in Prayer

What kind of fruit will we bear?

Prayer fruit, for one thing. Jesus promised if we would maintain living contact with Him and keep His Words alive in us, our prayers would produce results.

Some people try to minimize prayer failures by saying, "Well, that's just how God is. Sometimes He answers us by saying 'Yes' and sometimes He answers by saying 'No.'" That may sound very nice and "spiritual," but it contradicts the Words of Jesus. He said, *"If ye abide in me, and my words abide in you, ye shall ask what ye will, and it shall be done unto you."*

Jesus wasn't speaking idly. He meant every word of that promise. He intended for us to receive everything we ask for in prayer. But He prefaced that promise with two "ifs." (You always have to watch for the "ifs" in the Bible!) He said, "If you abide in Me, and if My words abide in you."

If you're maintaining living contact and union with Jesus, and His Word is alive and speaking to your heart, when you pray, you'll see results. You'll have the forces of life and faith coming out of you so that you will reach out into this natural world and change circumstances when you pray. Your faith will be strong.

Those who don't maintain that living contact won't experience that kind of prayer power. Spiritually they'll wither and become like those dead branches that men gather and cast into the fire. Instead of triumphing over the devil and the circumstances he brings them, the devil will triumph over them.

Christians who don't stay hooked up to God on a continual basis, who don't talk to Him and give attention to His Word, become a prey for Satan and his evil works. When he comes into their lives to kill, steal and destroy, they don't have the strength to overcome him. Even though according to the Word they are overcomers, in a time of trouble, they'll find themselves too weak to use the authority God has given them.

They may not be bad people. They may not deserve the destruction the devil brings them, but the devil doesn't give people what they deserve, he does whatever he can get away with. And when he finds a Christian who has broken his connection with God, he knows he can get away with plenty!

I heard one preacher say it this way: "If you give the devil a ride, pretty soon he'll be wanting to drive." That's the way the devil is. If you don't tell him what to do, he'll tell you what to do. If you let him get away with one thing, he'll try two.

So you just can't afford to give him an inch. *"Neither give place to the devil"* (Ephesians 4:27). You can't afford to miss your time with the Lord, because you need to be able at any moment to exercise the spiritual power that pushes the devil out of your way.

The Fruit of the Spirit

In addition to bearing prayer fruit, abiding in Jesus also enables us to bear all the fruit of the spirit. You can find them listed in Galatians 5:22-23. I especially like *The Amplified Bible* translation of those verses. It says:

The fruit of the (Holy) Spirit, [the work which His presence within accomplishes]—is love, joy (gladness), peace, patience (an even temper, forbearance), kindness, goodness (benevolence), faithfulness; (Meekness, humility) gentleness, self-control (self-restraint...).

All those fruit were put within you the moment you were born again. They will forever be a part of your reborn spirit because it is made in the image of God. He put His own, divine nature inside you, and the fruit of the spirit are characteristics of His nature.

But even though they are inside you, no matter how hard you work at it, you'll never be able to consistently manifest those fruit in your life unless you are abiding in Jesus, spending time daily in prayer and in the Word. Think about the illustration He gave of the vine and the branches, and you can easily see why that is.

The branch of an apple tree doesn't bear apples because it struggles and strives. It bears apples because it's united to the trunk of the tree, and the life within that tree flowing through the branch just naturally brings forth apples.

In the same way, when you're in union and communion with Jesus, the Vine, His divine life flows through you and produces spiritual fruit. Jesus is your Life Force! Your living contact with Him determines your spiritual results.

Of course, He won't grow the fruit *for* you any more than the apple tree will take up the responsibility of the branch and grow apples straight from the trunk of the tree. He simply provides you with the power and the life. Then you must do your part by choosing to yield to that life. By an act of your will, you must let that which Jesus has put on the inside of you manifest itself on the outside.

When someone says something ugly to you, for example, you have to make a decision. Will you yield to the irritation of your flesh and say something ugly in return? Or will you yield to your spirit and respond in love?

The answer to those questions will be determined by two factors. The first is, of course, the choice that you make. The second is the condition of your heart. If you have been daily abiding in fellowship with the Lord, then your heart will be strong and full of the spiritual energy necessary to overrule the flesh and let the love flow.

If you have been neglecting your time with God, however, spending more time in front of the television than in the Word, you may find yourself too weak to obey the voice of the Spirit. Although your heart's desire is to act lovingly, your flesh will win the struggle with your undernourished spirit and lash out in anger toward the one who wronged you.

Rules Have No Power

Later, no doubt, you would be sorry for your action and would probably resolve not to act again in such an ungodly way. You might even start to set up rules for yourself in order to curb your behavior.

Will such rules work? No, because if you aren't abiding in Jesus, you won't have the spiritual strength to keep them. And even if you did, you'd be making the same mistake the Christians in Galatia made.

The Galatians lost their hold on the grace of God. They stopped living by faith and started once again to live by Old Testament law. Instead of walking out their salvation through living contact with God, they were trying to walk it with their own natural strength and abilities.

The Apostle Paul wrote them and said:

O foolish Galatians, who hath bewitched you, that ye should not obey the truth, before whose eyes Jesus Christ hath been evidently set forth, crucified among you? This only would I learn of you, Received ye the Spirit by the works of the law, or by the hearing of faith? Are ye so foolish? having begun in the Spirit, are ye now made perfect by the flesh? (Galatians 3:1-3).

There is nothing unique about the Galatians. Many modern-day believers are unwittingly following in their footsteps. As a result, we continually see two methods of living the Christian life demonstrated in the Church today. As Bible scholar Kenneth Wuest says:

One (of these methods) is...dependence upon the Holy Spirit for the supply of both the desire and the power to do the will of God. This method results in a life in which the fruit of the spirit is evident. The other method is that of putting one's self under law, and by self effort attempting to obey that law. This results in a defeated life (Kenneth S. Wuest, *Wuest's Word Studies From the Greek New Testament,* Vol. I [Grand Rapids: Wm. B. Eerdmans Publishing Co., 1973], p. 163).

Many sincere believers find themselves in this position because they either don't know how to hear from the Holy Spirit and make the correct adjustments and yield to His strength, or they don't give God their attention so that they stay full of the Spirit. They're not availing themselves to the God-appointed method of living the Christian life which is union, a living contact.

God never intended the Christian life to be lived by a set of rules. He didn't want it to be lived by law. He wants us to have a heart for Him.

Do you know what living by the law is? It's doing something not because you want to, but because you're supposed to do it. It's attending church because it's the "right" thing to do, when you'd really rather be somewhere else.

That kind of living doesn't please God, even though it looks good to the eyes of men. If you think about it, you can understand why. How would you feel if someone did something nice for you, and then you found out that they didn't really want to do it? You wouldn't like it very much, would you?

How would you feel if someone came to visit you and you knew they really didn't come because they liked you and wanted to see you; they came because they felt legally or religiously obligated to do so? You'd probably prefer they'd just save themselves the effort and stay home.

Even so, the Father desires His children to fellowship with Him because they love Him and want Him in their lives.

The Christian Life Is Simple

God wants us to do the right thing. He wants us to come to church and act in love. He wants us to serve Him. But He wants us to do those things because we have a heartfelt desire to do them. And that takes us right back to living contact.

It's only by spending time with God that we develop those kinds of desires. The more we fellowship with Him, the more they grow.

I know it probably amazes worldly people (and even some religious people) when they see thousands of people come to our conventions and spend an entire week, all day and all evening, listening to the Word of God. Many of the believers who come use their vacation time to be able to do it.

No doubt, their co-workers say, "What?! You're planning to spend your entire vacation at church?" They think someone who would do that must either be crazy or have a tremendous amount of religious discipline. They can't imagine wanting to spend one day in church, much less a whole week. But the fact is, that's exactly what these believers want to do.

They don't come to hear the Word because they think they have to do it to satisfy some religious requirement. They do it because they'd rather be where the Word of God is being preached than anywhere else in the world! They've developed that desire by abiding in Jesus and spending time with Him.

Of course, not everyone who comes to our conventions is like that. There are always some who hear a little about faith, find out that if they'll act on the Word it will bring blessings into their life, and think, *Well, I'll try that.* So they listen to a tape or two and come to a few meetings and then try to put what they've learned into action, without ever establishing a lifestyle of living contact with God. They try to work faith like a formula. But faith is not a formula. It's living and walking every day with the Lord that makes faith work.

People like that eventually grow tired of trying to remember all the steps and make things work in their own strength, so they quit. "That faith stuff is too hard!" they'll say.

But they're mistaken. The life of faith isn't hard. In fact, as Rufus Moseley once wrote, "Life is gloriously easy when you walk in the Spirit."

Let this truth be written on your heart: *The Christian life is simple when you abide in Jesus through prayer and through the Word. When you don't—it's impossible.*

It doesn't matter if you've been saved and in the ministry for 25 years. It doesn't matter if you have great gifts of the Spirit operating in your life. If you stop having living contact with God on a daily basis, you'll begin to slip. Even though you know the right things to do, you won't be able to do them.

That's because living contact can't be stored up. It can't be learned like some dusty old doctrine and then put away. It has to be maintained continually. If you want to have a fruitful life, you must fellowship with Jesus every day.

4

It's More Than Possible...
It's Inevitable!

Abiding in the Vine doesn't just make it possible for you to bear spiritual fruit, it ensures you will bear fruit. That's right! If you abide and maintain a living connection with God—fruit is inevitable.

Jesus told us so in John 15:5. He said, *"I am the vine, ye are the branches: He that abideth in me, and I in him, the same bringeth forth much fruit...."* Notice Jesus didn't say, "If you abide in Me, you *might* bring forth fruit," or "If you abide in Me, you'll *probably* bring forth fruit." He said, "You *will!*" The fruit of the spirit always flourish when we maintain living fellowship with the Lord.

That's good news because the fruit of the spirit are more than just nice characteristics. They are powerful, supernatural forces, and if we want to live on this Earth in victory, we must have those forces at work in our lives.

Although I won't take the time here to examine in depth all the fruit of the spirit in this chapter (that would take a book in itself), I do want to look briefly at some of them, so you can see how they grow when we spend time in living contact with God.

Take joy, for example. Jesus mentioned it specifically when He talked to His disciples about abiding. He said, *"These things have I spoken unto you, that my joy might remain in you, and that your joy might be full"* (John 15:11).

What would keep their joy full? Abiding in the Vine, staying in contact and communion with Him.

The Apostle Paul echoed that truth in Colossians 2:7 when he said, *"See that you go on growing in the Lord, and become strong and vigorous in the truth you were taught. Let your lives overflow with joy..." (The Living Bible).*

Joy is an extremely important spiritual force. You must have it to live in this world as an overcomer because *"the joy of the Lord is your strength"* (Nehemiah 8:10), and without strength you can't win the battles of life.

The only place you can obtain joy is from God. Some people don't realize that. They think you can receive joy from the world. They're wrong. Natural things don't bring joy. They might bring you a moment of happiness. But even that will be fleeting at best, because the same world that makes you happy one moment, will turn on you and make you sad the next.

God is the only true generator of joy. It's one of His primary characteristics. If you're depressed, just start hanging around Him. The Bible says that *"in [His] presence is fulness of joy!"* (Psalm 16:11).

It may surprise you to hear this, but heaven is not a sad place. People are laughing there. They're singing and dancing and having a wonderful time because they're dwelling in the presence of God. They're full of the joy of the Lord.

But, praise God, we don't have to wait till we die to join in the fun! We can come into the presence of God while we're still in this natural body, because we are born of God and our citizenship is in heaven.

It's true! When you maintain a living connection with God, when you keep His Word abiding in your heart and fellowship with Him continually, you can have *"days of heaven upon the earth"* (Deuteronomy 11:21). Does that mean you won't have any problems? No, it simply means that when your circumstances aren't good, you don't have to be miserable about it. You can just maintain your union with the Lord and let His joy start bubbling up within you.

That joy will give you the strength you need to keep on walking in faith until the problem is solved.

Faithfulness, Love, Patience...and More

"But, Gloria," you may say, "I'm not just running short on joy these days, I'm also having trouble walking consistently in faith. I'm strong in the Lord one day...and weak the next."

No problem! Faithfulness is another fruit of the spirit that flourishes when you maintain a living connection with God. So if you're lacking in faithfulness, all you need to do is start spending time each day fellowshiping with the Lord in His Word.

The dictionary defines faithfulness as being "(1) full of faith; believing; strong or firm in one's faith, (2) firmly adhering to duty; of true fidelity, loyal, true to allegiance; constant in the performances of duties or services." To be faithful is to be trustworthy and dependable. If you want a perfect picture of faithfulness, look at God Himself for He is faithful! (1 Corinthians 1:9)

Actually, the Greek word for *faithfulness* used in the New Testament can also be translated *faith*. So faith and faithfulness are very closely related.

You might say it this way. Faith is faithfulness to God's Word. Faith is being faithful to believe what God says, even when circumstances, obstacles or people seem to contradict His Word.

Living contact causes you to grow in faithfulness. It strengthens you in your walk of faith so that you can reach out and receive the blessings of God, blessings like healing, prosperity and protection. Proverbs 28:20 promises, *"A faithful man shall abound with blessings."*

You see, everything we need in this life, Jesus has already bought for us with His blood. As Galatians 3:13-14 says:

Christ hath redeemed us from the curse of the law, being made a curse for us: for it is written, Cursed is every one that hangeth on a tree: That the blessing of Abraham might come on the Gentiles through Jesus Christ; that we might receive the promise of the Spirit through faith.

If you'll read Deuteronomy 28, you'll see that every good thing imaginable is included in God's blessing, and every bad thing imaginable is included in the curse. So we're set up in style! God has already provided everything we could ever need. We don't have to talk Him into giving us these things. They're already ours. The blessing has "come on" us!

All we have to do is put ourselves in a position to receive. And the primary key to receiving is faithfulness. We must be faithful to believe and faithful to act on the Word of God.

Of course, before you can even begin to believe God's Word, you must know what He has said. For faith comes *"by hearing, and hearing by the word of God"* (Romans 10:17). But to be faithful to that Word, you must do more than casually read it now and then. You must believe it and act on it consistently. And to do that, you must have confidence in the One Who spoke that Word. You must have confidence in God.

Such confidence is developed by spending time with Him. Just as you grow to trust another person (assuming he is a trustworthy person) by getting to know him better, by listening to him speak and deepening your relationship with him, so it is with God. The more time you spend with Him, the better you will know Him—and the better you know Him, the greater will be your confidence in Him.

That confidence will enable you to faithfully take God at His Word. You won't sit around wondering if He will do what He said. You won't believe Him one day and doubt Him the next. You'll be able to consistently believe and act like His Word is true even when circumstances indicate that it isn't.

When you're in living contact with God every day, you'll be able to look beyond the circumstances that are staring you in the face and screaming at you, *You'll go bankrupt!* or *You'll die young!* You'll have the strength of character to see past those circumstances and focus instead on the power and love of God and His ability to bring you through in victory.

In his book on the fruit of the spirit, Donald Gee illustrates wonderfully how living fellowship with the Spirit of God brings forth faithfulness in our lives. "Our human natures in all their unreliability (are like)...the loose power of cement," he says. "But when water is mixed with the cement it turns into concrete hard as a rock. So the living water of God's Holy Spirit can turn our lack of steadfastness into magnificent faithfulness, and convert many an impulsive 'Simon' into a devoted 'Peter'" (Donald Gee, *The Fruit of the Spirit* [Springfield: Gospel Publishing House, 1928], p. 60, used by permission of the publisher).

That, in itself, is reason enough to spend time every day in the Word and in prayer. But there are more reasons still!

Living contact with God will not cause just joy and faithfulness to flourish, it will cause all the rest of the fruit of the spirit to grow in your life too. It will empower you to walk with love, and that's vital because love never fails! (We'll talk more about love later.)

It will enable you to live in peace. It will also strengthen your ability to be patient. Patience is a powerful force that undergirds your faith and keeps you from quitting when tests and trials come. When patience is operating in your life, instead of succumbing to the pressure of circumstances, you can keep on believing God.

Freedom From Sin

In addition to all that, living contact with God will give you the power to be temperate, or self-controlled, and keep your body under subjection to your spirit so that your body will do what it's supposed to do. It will enable you to conquer strongholds of sin that for years may have been conquering you!

Some people expect to be free of such strongholds the moment they are born again. But, in most cases, acquiring that freedom is a process that takes place over time. That's because the new birth takes place in our spirit. It makes us new on the inside, but on the outside we have the same old body (and usually the same old habits) we've always had.

The challenge of the Christian life lies in bringing the salvation that's on the inside through to the outside. Our job is to follow the instructions in Ephesians 4:22-24:

> **Strip yourselves of your former nature—put off and discard your old unrenewed self—which characterized your previous manner of life and becomes corrupt through lusts and desires...And be constantly renewed in the spirit of your mind—having a fresh mental and spiritual attitude, And put on the new nature (the regenerate self) created in God's image, (Godlike) in true righteousness and holiness *(The Amplified Bible).*

We must learn, as the Apostle Paul said, to keep our body under and bring it into subjection to our reborn spirit (1 Corinthians 9:27). We must strengthen our spirit so it can take authority over the body and tell it what to do.

Living contact with God, in prayer and His written Word, helps us do that. When we spend time meditating on that Word, it works like spiritual food, strengthening our inner man so we can rise up on the inside and take dominion over those fleshly sins and weaknesses that hinder our life in God. It purifies us of ungodly thoughts, attitudes and behaviors, and keeps us abiding in Him. It keeps our thinking straight.

As Jesus said in John 15:

> **Every branch in me that beareth not fruit he taketh away:**

**and every branch that beareth fruit, he purgeth it, that
it may bring forth more fruit. Now ye are clean through
the word which I have spoken unto you (verses 2-3).**

Staying in contact with God through His Word cleanses
you from sin in two ways. First, by feeding your spirit and
second, by starving your carnal nature.

You see, the principle of living contact works both ways.
Just as the power and fruit of the spirit withers when you lose
your communion with God, the power of sin withers when
you maintain that communion.

As I said before, to wither means *to shrivel, to lose or cause
to lose energy, force or freshness.* When you maintain your
union with God, sin withers in your life. It has no force to
feed it and it shrivels up and dies.

So if you've been struggling with sin, cut off the devil's
influence in your life by turning your attention away from
worldly things and onto the Lord. Spend time every day fellowshiping with God in His Word. Spend time daily praying
and worshiping in God's presence.

Do what Colossians 3:2 says and *"Set your affection on
things above, not on things on the earth."* When you do that,
sin will lose its appeal and its power. You won't even be
tempted to do some of the things you used to do. And those
things you are tempted to do, you'll have the power to resist.
You'll have the spiritual strength flowing through you to follow the instructions in Romans 6:

**Even so consider yourselves also dead to sin and
your relation to it broken, but [that you are] alive to
God—living in unbroken fellowship with Him—in**

Christ Jesus. Let not sin therefore rule as king in your mortal...bodies, to make you yield to their cravings and be subject to their lusts and evil passions. Do not continue offering or yielding your bodily members [and faculties] to sin as instruments (tools) of wickedness. But offer and yield yourselves to God as though you have been raised from the dead to [perpetual] life, and your bodily members [and faculties] to God, presenting them as implements of righteousness. For sin shall not [any longer] exert dominion over you... (verses 11-14, *The Amplified Bible).*

Fellowshiping with God on a continual basis and maintaining a living connection with Him will enable you to keep your body under control, so that sin doesn't obtain a foothold in your life.

One of the best examples of that truth is one Ken often gives from his own life. He began smoking at a very young age. As he tells it, he thoroughly enjoyed smoking. But when he made Jesus the Lord of his life, he began wanting to break that habit.

The problem was, he couldn't. He tried and tried. He'd decide to quit while he was driving down the highway and would throw his cigarettes out the car window. A few minutes later, he'd turn the car around to go back and look for them. He was miserable about it.

Then he went down to Houston and spent three weeks in a meeting where the living Word of God was being preached. He spent all day every day listening to that Word and fellowshiping with the Lord.

Do you know what happened? He forgot about those cigarettes!

When the meeting was over, he sat down in his car to drive home and realized the cigarettes he'd left tucked above the visor were still there. He hadn't smoked one for days. That tobacco habit had withered and died. It no longer had the strength to control him. He was free!

Wouldn't you like to have that kind of freedom? Wouldn't it be wonderful if you were so abounding in the fruit of the spirit that the words that described you best were the ones found in Galatians 5:22?

Love, joy, peace, patience, kindness, goodness, faithfulness, gentleness and self-control—what a heavenly kind of life those forces would bring you. Such a life can actually be yours! The life of God flowing through you has the power to produce those fruit in you.

Looking at yourself right now you may wonder, *Is it really possible?*

It's more than possible, it's promised. If you abide in Jesus, it's inevitable.

5

Keep the Union

Once we understand the divine power that comes to us as we abide in Jesus, it is easy to see that if we want to live a victorious life, we must first and foremost maintain our union and communion with Him. That is without question our most important responsibility.

If we'll maintain that union, He'll take care of everything else. Unfortunately, however, many Christians do just the opposite. They become so busy maintaining the other things in their lives that they don't have time to spend with God. They spend their lives maintaining their houses and their lawns, their cars and their jobs. They even find time to maintain their hair and their fingernails. Yet they neglect the one thing that is vital to their life and well-being. They neglect their union with God.

Often they don't even realize it. They think that because they love the Lord and believe His Word, their union with Him is intact. But that's not necessarily so.

To be in union means to be joined together with something or someone. It's the act or instance of joining two or more things into one. Romans 7:4 likens our union with God to marriage. It says we've been married to Him. First Corinthians 6:17 further states that *"the person who is united to the Lord becomes one spirit with Him" (The Amplified Bible).* The word *united* used there (or *joined* in the *King James Version)* means *laminated.* It refers to something glued so tightly together that it becomes like one substance.

As we begin to spend time with the Lord, we begin to think like He thinks. We begin to act like He acts. We begin to hear from heaven moment by moment so that we can walk out the perfect will of God for our lives every day.

Our goal is to become so in tune with Him that when He tells us to do something, we hear Him and obey. Our aim is to be so closely joined to Him that the desires of our heart, the thoughts of our mind, the words of our mouth and our every action become a reflection of the One with Whom we are united.

That is God's desire too. For if He is to carry out His will in the Earth, He must have people who will join themselves with Him in that way. As Rufus Moseley wrote, "God has to have branches of the same texture as Himself, the same sap, the same mind, the same spirit, before He can bring forth in fullness what He wants to bring forth.... (So) keep the union. Put Him first and keep your mind stayed on Him in union and in love."

Perfect Union = Perfect Peace

How do you keep your mind stayed on God? By giving Him your attention. By putting His Word first place every day and focusing on it until it is the biggest thing in your life. *The Living Bible* says it this way:

Since you became alive again, so to speak, when Christ arose from the dead, now set your sights on the rich treasures and joys of heaven where he sits beside God in the place of honor and power. Let heaven fill your thoughts... (Colossians 3:1-2).

Spiritually speaking, when you received Jesus as your Lord, you died to this world and became alive to God. So you should have as little desire for this world as a dead person does!

You shouldn't spend your time worrying about worldly concerns. You should spend your time listening to what God has to say. You should keep your mind focused on Him.

Isaiah 26:3 says, *"Thou [God] wilt keep him in perfect peace, whose mind is stayed on thee...."* Jesus confirmed that when He said, *"Peace I leave with you, my peace I give unto you: not as the world giveth, give I unto you. Let not your heart be troubled, neither let it be afraid"* (John 14:27).

The world doesn't have any peace. If you keep your mind on the world and stay in union with it, you won't have any peace either. If you give the majority of your time and attention to worldly matters and secular entertainment, you will be carnally minded, and the Bible says, *"to be carnally minded is death; but to be spiritually minded is life and peace"* (Romans 8:6).

In other words, if you think like the world thinks, you'll receive the same results the world does. Instead of enjoying the healing power of God, you'll suffer with the sicknesses of the world. Instead of laying hold of heavenly prosperity, the depression, recession and poverty of the world will lay hold of you! Instead of being full of good news, you'll be full of bad news.

Contact with the wrong thing gives you the wrong results, and there are plenty of opportunities to be in contact with the world's way of thinking. In the United States, it's possible to watch the news 24 hours a day. (It's a terrible curse, but you can do it.) You can turn on the television any time of the day or night and hear about all the things the devil is doing.

"Well, Gloria," you say, "we can't stick our heads in the sand. We have to face the facts."

I'm not suggesting we stick our heads in the sand. I'm suggesting we keep them in the Word!

I am also suggesting that sometimes the news doesn't give us the facts. I watch the news, but I'm careful about what I believe from the world's voice. God's voice is my authority.

A few years ago, for example, the media announced that the United States' economy was in recession. For about a year and a half, they talked about the recession. News of the recession influenced the elections that year. It influenced everything that happened because the media constantly broadcast it.

Sometime later a statistical report came out that revealed the recession had actually lasted only a few months. Why, then, had the news media kept on reporting about it? They didn't know it had ended. They were in the dark so they kept screaming, "Recession! Recession!" even though the recession had been over for more than a year.

Thank heaven, that recession never got off the ground with us. When news of it first came out, the Lord spoke to Ken and said, *Write your Partners and tell them not to join the recession.* So we obeyed God and didn't get in on that recession. We just let it pass us by.

That may sound strange to you, but as citizens of heaven, you and I can do that kind of thing. If we stay in union with God, we don't have to be dependent on this world's economy. We can be hooked up to heaven's economy, and there's no recession, depression or inflation there. In God's economy there's no shortage or lack of any kind. He is our shepherd, we shall not want (Psalm 23:1)!

If you unite with the world's voice, you'll always be in trouble, because the world is always in trouble. But if you'll spend your time listening to what God says and maintain your union with Him, if you'll keep your mind stayed on the Word of God no matter what the news media says, and no matter what the circumstances say, God will deliver you from any trouble. The Lord told my friend Lynne Hammond, *If you'll give Me enough time (meaning spend enough time with Me), I can turn anything around for you.* He'll meet your needs, not according to the government, not according to what happens in this natural economy, but according to His riches in glory!

The circumstances on this Earth don't bother God. He's not bound by them or limited to them. He can prosper you any time, anywhere and in any way He wants.

God knows how to prosper people even when they're in slavery! Read the book of Exodus and you can see that for yourself. He brought the Israelites out of slavery in Egypt with silver and gold. The Bible says they plundered the Egyptians, because the Egyptians loaded them with treasure and sent them out of the country as rich people!

You're Connected!

It doesn't matter how bad things become out there in the world. You aren't in the world without a Savior! You are *"connected to Christ, the Head to which all of us who are his body are joined"* (Colossians 2:19, *The Living Bible*).

When someone has friends in high places, we sometimes say, "He's connected." Well, if you're maintaining living contact with God, you're connected! You're connected with the highest ruler and authority in existence. You have a connection with the power above every other power, and you need to maintain an awareness of that connection. You ought to think about it all through the day.

If you'll do that, then the faith and power of God will rise up within you to deal with whatever comes your way. Even if it's danger of the worst kind, you'll be ready.

One of our Partners proved that fact in her own life a few years ago. She was traveling on a bus in a major city she was visiting, and some men aboard that bus began to rob people. They were going from one person to the next taking money, jewelry and other valuables.

But this lady had been maintaining her union with the Lord. She was strong on the inside and had His power flowing through her. So when the thieves came to her, something happened. Instead of cowering in fear and handing over her possessions, she looked those men straight in the eye and said, "In the Name of Jesus, you take your hands off me!"

Suddenly it didn't matter that those men were armed. It didn't matter that they were much bigger than she was. Whatever happened in the spirit realm when she spoke those faith words scared those men so badly, they not only left her alone—they ran off that bus!

You may be a 100-pound woman or a 250-pound man. Your physical stature is irrelevant. You become a giant when you're connected to Jesus. You're unbeatable when you're hooked up with Him. If you'll maintain a living connection with the Lord, whatever you do, wherever you go, the power of God will be just one breath away.

We live in a day when you may need that power at any moment. We're living in the last of the last days, and there is danger all around us. When that danger strikes, we may not have time to go find our Bible and look up a scripture about protection. We need to have the Word in our heart. We need to have it dwelling in us so richly that it comes up in us before we even have time to think.

In times of crisis, your mind usually goes blank, and whatever is in your heart comes out. If you've been fellowshiping with the world, fear will come out. If you've been fellowshiping with God, faith will come out. In times of trouble that will make all the difference.

6

Let the Word Abide in You

Although we fellowship with God in a number of ways, the primary avenue through which we have living contact with Him is through His written Word.

Why do I consider the Word the most important? Because the Bible says that without faith it is impossible to please God (Hebrews 11:6), therefore, all our dealings with God must be based on faith. And since faith comes by hearing, and hearing by the Word of God (Romans 10:17), the Word provides the foundation for all divine contact.

Take prayer, for example. It is a very important form of fellowship with God. There's no denying that. But faith is essential if you want your prayers to be answered. To have an effective prayer life, you have to know what God has said and believe it. In Mark 11:24 Jesus said, *"What things soever ye desire, when ye pray, believe that ye receive them, and ye shall have them."*

It is impossible to pray effectively without a knowledge of God's Word, because for the most part, prayers that are not based on the Word are prayers of unbelief. I proved that in my own life. I prayed at various times throughout my early years, but because I didn't hear the Word until I was a grown woman, most of my prayers were just a rehearsal of the problem.

God already knew the problem! What He needed was for me to open the door of faith, so He could move into my life and solve that problem. But I didn't have any faith. I didn't believe I received when I prayed according to Mark 11:24.

So what happened as a result of those faithless prayers? For the most part, nothing at all.

"But Gloria," you ask, "couldn't you have prayed for faith?"

Yes, I could have, but I wouldn't have received any that way because faith doesn't come by praying. It comes by hearing the Word of God. The only way you can obtain faith is to hear the Word preached or take it yourself and spend time in it!

Of course, you can spend a lifetime studying the Word like a textbook just to gain natural knowledge, just to learn facts, and it won't generate faith or do anything else for you spiritually. For the Word to be effective in your life, you have to let it become more than just a book to you. You must treat it as though God is speaking to you personally through its pages. You must let God's Words jump out of your Bible and into your heart, so they can abide and take up residence there.

God's Words can do that because they're not just tired, dead, old phrases. They are supernatural words that originated in heaven. As Hebrews 4:12 says:

The Word that God speaks is alive and full of power—making it active, operative, energizing and effective; it is sharper than any two-edged sword, penetrating to the dividing line of the breath of life (soul) and [the immortal] spirit, and of joints and marrow [that is, of the deepest parts of our nature] exposing and sifting and analyzing and judging the very thoughts and purposes of the heart *(The Amplified Bible).*

God's Words had life in them the moment He first spoke them. And even though they've been written down in a Book for thousands of years, those Words are still as powerful and full of life as they were the day God spoke them. His Words are eternal. Jesus said they are spirit and they are life (John 6:63). So when you take the Words that are in that Book and put them in your heart and in your mouth, it brings supernatural things to pass.

God's Word makes a circle. It comes down to us from Him like rain from heaven and goes into the soil of our hearts (Mark 4). Then we lift those Words back up to Him by faith in prayer, and He brings them to pass in our lives.

Isaiah 55:10-11 says it like this:

As the rain and snow come down from the heavens, and return not there again, but water the earth and make it bring forth and sprout, that it may give seed to the sower and bread to the eater, So shall My word be that goes forth out of My mouth; it shall not return to Me void—without producing any effect, useless—but it shall accomplish that which I please and purpose, and it shall prosper in the thing for which I sent it *(The Amplified Bible).*

Keep the Word Alive in You

Remember though, if you want the Word to produce those kinds of powerful results in your life, you can't be content just to "know" it. You must believe it and meditate on it until it abides in you so that you will obey it—we call that acting on the Word. First John 2:24 says it this way:

> **As for you, keep in your hearts what you have heard from the beginning. If what you heard from the first dwells and remains in you, then you will dwell in the Son and in the Father (always)** *(The Amplified Bible).*
>
> **For yourselves, let the teaching which you have heard from the beginning abide within you. If that teaching does abide within you, you also will abide in the Son and in the Father** *(The New Testament in Modern Speech,* **Richard Francis Weymouth).**

The secret to the abiding life is to put the Word into your heart in abundance, so it will dwell and come alive in you! You must give your attention to it just like God instructed Joshua to do in Joshua 1. You must:

> **Turn not from it to the right hand or to the left, that you may prosper wherever you go. This book... shall not depart out of your mouth, but you shall meditate on it day and night, that you may observe and do according to all that is written in it; for then you shall make your way prosperous, and then you shall deal wisely and have good success (verses 7-8,** *The Amplified Bible).*

I realize, of course, that you can't walk around reading your Bible 24 hours a day. But if you're committed to abiding in the Word, you'll find ways to put it into your heart. You can certainly keep the Word abiding in you 24 hours a day.

Ken and I first learned to walk by faith back in the 1960s by listening to tapes by Brother Kenneth Hagin. Back then we didn't have the convenient little cassette tapes that are available now. We had to use the big 7-inch reel-to-reel kind.

Every day I'd hurry and finish my housework so that I could sit down and listen to those tapes. I listened to them so many times and took so many notes, I eventually wrote down word for word a great part of those tapes. I still have my notebook today.

In addition, whenever Brother Hagin held a meeting there in Tulsa, we found a way to be there. I believe in the year we lived there, he held four 10-day meetings and we didn't miss one of them. We had to slip and slide our way over ice-covered streets to attend some of them, but we did it because we were so desperate for the Word!

That desperation paid off too. Before long, things in our life began to change. Because we started abiding in the Word, the Word started abiding in us.

How do you know if the Word is abiding in you? It begins to speak to you. If the Word is not talking to you, then it's not alive in you and you need to freshen your remembrance of it. Proverbs 6:20-22 says:

My son, keep thy father's commandment, and forsake not the law of thy mother: Bind them continually upon thine heart, and tie them about thy neck. When thou goest, it shall lead thee...and when thou awakest, it shall talk with thee.

The Word that's abiding in you, the Word that's alive in you, is the Word that talks to you. It's the Word that leads you moment by moment as you go about your day. The abiding Word will come up in your heart unexpectedly, much like the words and notes of a familiar song might waft spontaneously through your mind.

The Word that's in you in abundance is also the Word that you hear coming out of your mouth, for out *"of the abundance of the heart [the] mouth speaketh"* (Luke 6:45). If you are in a situation where you need a scripture to come out of your mouth and you find yourself speaking doubt and fear instead, that's an indication the Word you need to overcome that situation is not alive in you.

To conquer the challenges of the devil, you must have the spiritual strength within you that only the engrafted Word can provide. You have to be so established in that Word that it automatically rises up within you at the moment of crisis. You have to be like the "young men" the Apostle John wrote to saying, *"Ye are strong, and the word of God abideth in you, and ye have overcome the wicked one"* (1 John 2:14).

No Deposit/No Return

If the Word is not abiding in you as it should, if it's not coming up inside you when you need it, the solution is simple. Spend more time in it. Put more of the Word in your heart...and more will come out!

In some ways your heart is like a bank account. If you want to write faith checks on that account, you must have plenty of Word in there to back them. Jesus said, *"A good man out of the good treasure of his heart bringeth forth that which* is good..." (Luke 6:45). Or, as Matthew 12:33-35 says in the *New International Version, "Make a tree good and its fruit will be good, or make a tree bad and its fruit will be bad, for a tree is recognized by its fruit. You brood of vipers, how can you who are evil say anything good? For out of the overflow of the heart the mouth speaks. The good man brings good things out of the good stored up in him, and the evil man beings evil things out of the evil stored up in him."*

If you haven't put money in the bank, when you write a check, money will not come out of the bank. The Word is the same way. If you haven't deposited God's Word about healing in your heart, when you become sick, words of healing will not come out of your mouth. If you haven't deposited God's Word about prosperity in your heart, when the devil attacks your finances, you won't have the spiritual funds to fight back.

"But I did deposit God's Word about healing in my heart," you say. "I read healing scriptures every day back in 1990."

You probably deposited a thousand dollars in the bank a few years ago too—but are you living on that money today? Of course not! It's long gone. You cashed checks on it and used it all.

By the same token, in this life you have to walk by faith, so you are continually writing faith checks. The Word you put inside you is made strength and produces faith (if you believe it and keep it), and you're continually drawing on that supply of strength to meet the challenges that come your way. You are always encountering situations that require supernatural help. So, to keep your strength account from running low, you must continually make deposits of the Word. You must keep a fresh deposit of the Word in your heart at all times by putting it in every day.

Right now you may not be in a position to make huge

deposits of money into your natural bank account. But you can make any size deposit you want to make in your heart account—and that's the account that really matters, because it's the one you must draw on to change the circumstances in your life. It holds the faith you'll need to cover any bill the devil tries to send your way.

When you're first starting your faith account, it's wise to begin making deposits in the area of your greatest need. If your biggest problem is finances, for example, you should set your attention on the Word of God concerning prosperity. You ought to go to the Word and start the power of God working in you, so faith will rise up in your heart and cause you to prosper.

Some people think that's selfish, but it's not. God wants to help you with your needs. He loves you. He wants to ease your distresses and supply your needs in every area. He wants to help you solve your problems—whether those problems are in your pocketbook, your family, your body or any other part of your life.

God is your Father. He feels about you the same way you feel about your children. Don't you want to bless your children? Don't you want to help them? Well, so does God! His heart is tender toward His children, and He is always looking for opportunities to bless them.

So give Him an opportunity! Open the door of faith for Him by spending time in His Word. Meditate on it until that Word becomes bigger inside you than the circumstances that surround you. Set your attention on the Word that gives you an answer to the problem you're facing, then focus on God's answer until you can look right past the circumstances and into the realm of the spirit. Focus on it until you can see God's Word coming to pass for you!

When you do that, you'll find that poverty and lack, sickness and failure of every kind will wither. They will lose their energy to stay in your life, and the provision of God will gain energy and bring you what you need.

By building your faith account, you'll bankrupt the devil in your life. He just won't have the resources to keep you down anymore. If he tries to put sickness on you, you can draw on the Word of God about healing and it will give you victory in that area.

But remember, you can't make a withdrawal from an account that doesn't have anything in it. No deposit, no return!

Some people don't understand that. They see someone else having their circumstances turned around by faith and they think, *Well, faith worked for that person, so I'll just do what he did and it will work for me too.*

That's not necessarily true. You may know someone who can write a check for a million dollars too, but that doesn't mean you can do it. It depends on whether you've put that much money in your bank account.

If you need more faith in your heart to meet the challenges you're facing right now, put some in there. Since faith comes by hearing the Word, you can have as much as you want. However much Word you put in your heart, that's how much faith you will have.

But remember this, no one can make deposits in your heart account but you. Your spouse can't do it for you. Your pastor can't do it for you. Even God can't do it for you. You're the one who has to open your Bible every day. You're the one who has to put in that teaching tape, go to that meeting where the Word is being preached and attend that church where the Word is being preached. You're the one who has to open your ears and your heart and receive the living Word!

When the Word Is Abiding in You, You'll Speak in Faith

One reason it's so important to have the Word abiding in you in abundance is that when you come up against a test or a trial, the devil will put tremendous pressure on you to say negative things. You'll find yourself strongly tempted to speak the problem instead of the Word. But you can't do that and come out in victory.

In Mark 11:23, Jesus taught us that *"whosoever shall say...and shall not doubt in his heart, but shall believe that those things which he saith shall come to pass; he shall have whatsoever he saith."* The realm of the spirit works according to our words. We have what we say. Our words are our faith speaking.

The devil knows that, so when our circumstances are bad, he pushes us to say what we have! He wants us to say, "I feel so sick!" instead of "By Jesus' stripes I am healed." He wants us to say, "I'm broke!" instead of "My God meets my needs according to His riches in glory."

Ken and I were in an elevator some time ago at a hotel. We stood in that elevator talking for a while but we didn't go anywhere. Then we realized we'd pushed the button of the floor that we were already on instead of pushing the button of the floor we wanted. That didn't take us anywhere!

As believers, most of us do the same thing with our words. We say what we have instead of saying what we desire. As a result, things just stay the way they are.

Even if we know we should be speaking the Word, when the pressure of adverse circumstances hits us, we won't be able to say what we should unless we're abiding in the Word, and the Word is abiding in us. We may even have to double up and give twice as much time and attention to the Word when we're in especially serious situations. I have a friend who had terminal cancer. She gave *all* her time to the Word of God until cancer had to depart.

There have been times in my life when the Spirit of God instructed me to go on a veritable "Word Binge." (That's my term, not His.) Do you know what a binge is? It's doing a whole lot of something. For example, when you go on a food binge, you eat almost anything you can get your hands on. You eat...and eat...and eat.

That's what I do with the Word when I'm on a Word binge. I don't watch any secular television or anything else that's not absolutely necessary. I spend all my free time reading the Word, listening to teaching tapes, reading good, Bible-based books or watching Christian television. And I continue doing that as long as the Lord directs. Actually, it would be a wise and powerful way to live all the time. However much time and attention we give God, that is how much blessing and anointing comes back to us.

In times past when He's instructed me to attend to the Word with such intensity, it was because there was a test or trial ahead of me that I didn't know was coming. He wanted me to be extra-full of the Word, so I'd be strong and ready for it.

So I suggest that you listen to the Lord when He gives you instructions like that. When He says to you, *Turn off the television for a few weeks and spend your evenings in the Word,* don't argue with Him. Just do it. He may tell you to put aside things that aren't sinful, just unnecessary. He may ask you to set aside some hobby or recreational activity and use that time to build up your spirit with the Word of God, because He knows you will need extra strength in the days to come.

Even when you haven't sensed a special prompting of the Lord to spend extra hours in the Word, be faithful to spend some time in it every day. Make abiding in the Word your permanent lifestyle so that His Word can abide in you. Open the way for it to make lasting changes in you and your circumstances by building the truth of it into your spirit day after day. Let it become engrafted in you to such a degree that it becomes a part of you. According to Jesus in John 15:7, you will ask what you will and it will be done. That is a great investment of your time!

That doesn't happen overnight. It takes time.

From the first day Ken and I began to walk by faith, our lives began to improve. But it took a while for us to lay hold of the Word of God to such an extent that it could significantly change our circumstances. It took time for the Word to work its way down into our hearts, take root there to take over our minds and mouths, and then become fruitful.

So don't become impatient. Don't expect to revolutionize your entire life in a day or two. Give the Word time to work. If you do, your life will never be the same.

7

Abiding Is Obeying

As important as it is to spend time reading, meditating and listening to God's Word, those things alone do not qualify you as one who abides. To be a true "abider" you must take one more step. You must not only hear the Word, you must act on it.

Abiding is obeying. As Jesus said:

He that hath my commandments, and keepeth them, he it is that loveth me: and he that loveth me shall be loved of my Father, and I will love him, and will manifest myself to him.... If a man love me, he will keep my words: and my Father will love him, and we will come unto him, and make our abode with him.... If ye keep my commandments, ye shall abide in my love; even as I have kept my Father's commandments, and abide in his love.... This is my commandment, That ye love one another, as I have loved you (John 14:21, 23, 15:10, 12).

There are a great many people who claim to know God. They can quote long passages of scripture and may even spend years in seminary studying the Bible. Yet they are deceived because they are not doers of the Word; they are hearers only (James 1:22).

The Word that is truly alive in us is not the Word we know, but the Word we *do*. First John 2:3-6 says it this way:

And hereby we do know that we know him, if we keep his commandments. He that saith, I know him, and keepeth not his commandments, is a liar, and the truth is not in him. But whoso keepeth his word, in him verily is the love of God perfected: hereby know we that we are in him. He that saith he abideth in him ought himself also to walk, even as he walked.

If we're abiding in Jesus, we will live as He lived.
How did He live? In obedience!
He was obedient to God in all things. He wouldn't even say anything except what the Father told Him to say.

"For I came down from heaven, not to do mine own will, but the will of him that sent me" (John 6:38). Jesus didn't live His life for Himself. He lived it to fulfill the Word and plan of His Father. He lived to be obedient.

Do you know how God responded to that obedience? He gave Jesus His Spirit without measure (see John 3:34). As a result, Jesus walked the Earth in total victory. He defeated Satan and destroyed his works at every turn. Everywhere He went, He made the blind see, the lame walk and the deaf hear. He cast out demons and raised the dead.

The world tries to convince us that it's more exciting to sin than to obey God. But Jesus proved that it's not. He lived the most exciting life in history.

Obeying God won't doom you to a life of boredom. Obeying God won't cheat you out of the good things of life. No! Obedience will lead you into the most thrilling life of victory and blessing you could ever imagine.

God desires to pour His power through you just as He poured it through Jesus. He desires to give you everything you ask for in prayer. He wants to bring to pass in your life the promise Jesus made in John 14:12-15:

> **Verily, verily, I say unto you, He that believeth on me, the works that I do shall he do also; and greater works than these shall he do; because I go unto my Father. And whatsoever ye shall ask in my name, that will I do, that the Father may be glorified in the Son. If ye shall ask any thing in my name, I will do it. If ye love me, keep my commandments.**

All too often, Christians quote those first three verses and leave out the last one. But that won't work. If we want to do the works of Jesus, we must live as He lived. We must abide in Him. And abiding is obeying His commandments.

Go in Love

As we saw in John 15:12, Jesus summed up those commandments with one statement: *"Love one another."* The Apostle John, while addressing the issue of answered prayer in 1 John 3:21-23, echoes His Words:

Beloved, if our consciences (our hearts) do not accuse us—if they do not make us feel guilty and condemn us—we have confidence (complete assurance and boldness) before God; And we receive from Him whatever we ask for, because we (watchfully) obey His orders—observe His suggestions and injunctions, follow His plan for us—and (habitually) practice what is pleasing to Him. And this is His order (His command, His injunction), that we should believe—put our faith and trust in and adhere to and rely—on the name of His Son Jesus Christ, the Messiah, and that we should love one another, just as He has commanded us *(The Amplified Bible).*

Beloved, if our hearts do not condemn us, we address God with confidence; and whatever we ask for we obtain from Him, because we obey His commands and do what is pleasing in His sight. And this is His command—that we are to believe in the name of His Son Jesus Christ and love one another, as He has commanded us to do *(The New Testament in Modern Speech,* Richard Francis Weymouth).

The love of God is our commandment. Obeying that commandment, living a lifestyle of love, is essential if you want to maintain living contact with God. First John 4:16 says, *"God is love, and he who dwells and continues in love dwells and continues in God, and God dwells and continues in him" (The Amplified Bible).* Every step out of love is a step out of this vital, living contact with God because you are walking in disobedience.

Years ago, Rufus Moseley wrote that if we live by the commandment of love, God's presence will always be with us. He said:

> I knew this was the secret. If we abide in His love and always go in love, feeling and willing and giving out nothing but love and all possible love to all men and all things, we will always be in Him and under His anointing. It was made known to me that I could write editorials and do everything else that can be done in the loving Spirit of Jesus. I could even be in heavenly places while plowing with a mule, pruning trees, in courtrooms, in death cells, in all places of need, provided all was done in the spirit of love (J. Rufus Moseley, *Manifest Victory* [Plainfield, N.J.: Logos International, 1971], p. 117).

Exactly what is the spirit of love? How does it display itself? First Corinthians 13 gives us a clear answer to those questions. It says:

Love endures long and is patient and kind; love never is envious nor boils over with jealousy; is not boastful or vainglorious, does not display itself haughtily. It is not conceited—arrogant and inflated with pride; it is not rude (unmannerly), and does not act unbecomingly. Love [God's love in us] does not insist on its own rights or its own way, for it is not self-seeking; it is not touchy or fretful or resentful; it takes no account of the evil done to it—pays no attention to a suffered wrong. It does not rejoice at injustice

and unrighteousness, but rejoices when right and truth prevail.

Love bears up under anything and everything that comes, is ever ready to believe the best of every person, its hopes are fadeless under all circumstances, and it endures everything [without weakening]. Love never fails... (verses 4-8, *The Amplified Bible).*

We must meditate and act on the revelation of love that comes through these verses until this God-kind-of love dominates our thought life and our every response to meanness, selfishness, every kind of persecution and hurt. God's love shed abroad in our hearts by the Holy Ghost never fails when we respond to it. Thank God for the fruit of our reborn spirit created in His image.

You're Not on Your Own

If you're sitting there thinking you could never consistently live a life of love, that it would simply be too hard for you, don't worry. None of us could do it on our own. But, thank God, we're not on our own! The Greater One is in us. It's His strength within us that makes us victorious.

Because God's own Spirit lives inside us, constantly empowering us to do His will, obedience isn't a burden—it's a joy! First John 5:3-4 confirms that saying:

For the [true] love of God is this, that we do His commands—keep His ordinances and are mindful of His precepts and teaching. And these orders of His are not irksome—burdensome, oppressive, or grievous.

For whatever is born of God is victorious over the world; and this is the victory that conquers the world, even our faith *(The Amplified Bible).*

If you're a born-again child of God, you *are* an overcomer. You may not be overcoming right now, but you have what it takes on the inside to overcome. So step into that overcoming lifestyle by spending time in the Word developing your faith, and in prayer fellowshiping with your Father. Talk to Him. Listen to Him. Depend on Him.

Allow the Word to change how you see yourself. Maybe you've suffered from low self-esteem all your life. Maybe you've been abused or criticized so much that you think of yourself as a failure. If so, stop focusing on yourself, and turn your focus on the Word of God instead. Begin to see yourself as the Father sees you. Whatever He says about you as His child, that's the way it really is. All you have to do is come into agreement with Him. He's God!

When you become hooked up to the Word of God, you'll be cured of low self-esteem. You won't see yourself in failure any longer. You'll see yourself in God!

You'll begin to read words like, *"Behold, what manner of love the Father hath bestowed upon us, that we should be called the sons of God..."* (1 John 3:1). You'll begin to see by revelation of the Spirit that God actually is your Father. He does care for you. You are recreated in Christ Jesus. All those failures of the past have passed away and all things have become new.

You'll realize that you are in God and He is in you. Then, when the devil of low self-esteem comes to you and says, *You'll never be able to obey God. You're not strong enough.*

You're not able, you'll answer him and say, "That's right. I'm not able in myself. My self needs God! And I have Him living here inside me. So get out of the way, devil, I'm an overcomer because THE GREATER ONE LIVES IN ME!"

8

Developing Confidence
in the Holy Spirit

Ye are of God, little children, and have overcome...because
greater is he that is in you, than he that is in the world
(1 John 4:4).

To enjoy real day-by-day, moment-by-moment living
contact with God, it is essential that we develop a deeper faith
in the Greater One Who is living within us. We must cultivate
an awesome appreciation for the indwelling Holy Spirit. We
must come to see Him like John G. Lake did, as "a reward so
great that Jesus Himself considered it worth all His sufferings,
all His buffetings, His Earth career, His humiliation, His sacrifice and death. All to obtain it, the GIFT OF THE HOLY SPIRIT"
(John G. Lake—His Life, His Sermons, His Boldness of Faith, rev.
ed. [Fort Worth: Kenneth Copeland Publications, 1994], p. 59).

Truly, the Holy Spirit is the greatest gift Jesus ever gave us! The Holy Spirit was the One upon Whom the disciples were instructed to pin their hope during the dark hours before Jesus' crucifixion. The Holy Spirit was the One Jesus spoke to them about in those last precious moments, saying:

> **Whither I go, thou canst not follow me now; but thou shalt follow me afterwards.... And I will pray the Father, and he shall give you another Comforter, that he may abide with you for ever; even the Spirit of truth; whom the world cannot receive, because it seeth him not, neither knoweth him: but ye know him; for he dwelleth with you, and shall be in you. I will not leave you comfortless: I will come to you.... These things have I spoken unto you, being yet present with you. But the Comforter, which is the Holy Ghost, whom the Father will send in my name, he shall teach you all things, and bring all things to your remembrance, whatsoever I have said unto you (John 13:36, 14:16-18, 25-26).**

To understand the impact of these words, you must realize that for three years, Jesus had been everything to His disciples. He'd been their teacher. He'd been their provider. When they had moments of fear and weakness, Jesus strengthened them. When they were confused, He counseled them. When they didn't know what to do or where to go, He gave them direction.

Those were the things they had in mind when they heard Him say, "I'm leaving but I'm not leaving you helpless. I'm sending Someone to take My place, Someone to act in My behalf, Someone to do everything for you that I have been doing. It will even be better than having Me here with you in the flesh."

No doubt, the disciples must have thought, *How could anyone do for us what You have done, Jesus?* They must have been stunned by sorrow and grief at the prospect of being without Him.

But Jesus didn't share that perspective. He didn't say, "I'm sorry, guys. I know things won't be as good for you after I'm gone, but the Holy Spirit will help you muddle through somehow."

No! Jesus said something far different. He said:

> **Because I have said these things to you sorrow has filled your hearts—taken complete possession of them. However, I am telling you nothing but the truth when I say, it is profitable—good, expedient, advantageous—for you that I go away. Because if I do not go away, the Comforter (Counselor, Helper, Advocate, Intercessor, Strengthener, Standby) will not come to you—into close fellowship with you. But if I go away, I will send Him to you—to be in close fellowship with you (John 16:6-7, *The Amplified Bible*).**

Don't ever desire to be like the first disciples. Don't ever think it would be easier to walk in faith and in living contact with God if Jesus were physically by your side. He said it's better, more advantageous and more profitable to have the Holy Spirit inside you! You're far better off than the disciples were during Jesus' earthly ministry. For the same Holy Spirit Who equipped and empowered Jesus Himself is now resident within you to equip and empower you.

Supernatural Counsel 24 Hours a Day

"Well, Gloria, I just can't see how anything could be better than walking with Jesus on the shores of Galilee like Peter and John did."

Sure you can! Think about it for a moment. When Jesus was on Earth, He had to divide His time between His disciples. He couldn't be everywhere at once. He couldn't be teaching and counseling each one of them 24 hours a day.

But the Holy Spirit can. He can be there when we wake up in the morning, fellowship with us all day long, put us to bed at night and be there while we sleep. If we wake up at 2 a.m. with a need or a question, He's there. No matter what time of the day or night we need Him, He's always available to us.

The Holy Spirit dwelling within us is our direct connection to God. He enables us to stay in continual fellowship and union with God. We don't have to go to the high priest to ask forgiveness. We don't have to go to some clergyman or church building to be in touch with God. We can just go to Him directly, any moment of the day or night. We can stay in contact with heaven all the time.

The Bible says if you are a born-again believer, you are a mobile temple of God! *"Your body is the temple—the very sanctuary—of the Holy Spirit Who lives within you, Whom you have received [as a Gift] from God"* (1 Corinthians 6:19, *The Amplified Bible*).

You never have to wonder, *God, where are You?* You never have to check your feelings to see if God is close to you or a million miles away. You can know He is right there inside you every moment of the day—whether you feel Him or not—because the Word says so.

He's not just along for the ride, either. He is there to teach you what you need to know. He's there to be your Counselor. And what a wonderful Counselor He is! He knows the answer to every problem you'll ever have, and because of that you can have peace even in the midst of a troubled world.

It doesn't matter how much trouble you're in, you'll never ask the Holy Spirit for help and hear Him say, "Oh, I don't know. That's a tough one. What can I say? You'll have to come back later because you've come up with a problem so complicated, I don't know the answer to it."

No, if you're in trouble, God always has a way out. If He has a way into your life, He can provide you with a way out of any problem. You'll never find Him not knowing what to do.

If you had a human counselor who was that smart, a natural person who knew the answer to every problem you had, you'd keep his telephone number written on your heart, wouldn't you? If you could just call him every time you ran into trouble and he could tell you what to do to straighten out the situation, you'd be on the phone to him a hundred times a day!

Of course, there's no human being with that kind of wisdom and power. But if you're filled with the Holy Spirit, you do have a Counselor like that. You have Someone Who *"will guide you into all truth...and he will show you things to come"* (John 16:13). You don't even have to call Him on the telephone. He's just there for you all the time. Through Him, any hour of the day or night, you always have living contact with God.

Find Out How God Thinks

Think of the opportunity we have! Through the indwelling Holy Spirit, we have the privilege of fellowshiping with

Almighty God—the highest ruler with authority over every other power. You can't spend time with the highest authority—the wisest, most loving, kindest, most generous One in the universe, and it not affect you greatly. You can't spend time in the presence of the Lord and just stay the same natural person. The more time you give Him, the more you will be like Him. Second Corinthians 3:17-18 says:

> **Now the Lord is the Spirit, and where the Spirit of the Lord is, there is liberty—emancipation from bondage, freedom. And all of us, as with unveiled face, [because we] continued to behold [in the Word of God] as in a mirror the glory of the Lord, are constantly being transfigured into His very own image in ever increasing splendor and from one degree of glory to another; [for this comes] from the Lord [Who is] the Spirit _(The Amplified Bible)._**

Colossians 3:10 says, _"Put on the new man, which is renewed in knowledge after the image of him that created him."_

Fellowship with God builds you up. It allows you to find out how God thinks. If you'll let Him, the Spirit of God living within your spirit will reveal to you the inside of God, the heart of the Father. He will show you God's plan for your life, then teach you how to walk in that plan step by step. He will give you the wisdom to be a success in every area of your life.

First Corinthians 2:9-10 says:

> **What eye has not seen, and ear has not heard, and has not entered into the heart of man, [all that,] God has prepared—made and keeps ready—for those who**

love Him.... Yet to us God has unveiled and revealed them by and through His Spirit, for the (Holy) Spirit searches diligently, exploring and examining everything, even sounding the profound and bottomless things of God... *(The Amplified Bible).*

As amazing as it may seem, those verses tell us clearly that the bottomless things of God are available to every Christian who will spend time with this wonderful Counselor! Yet instead of taking advantage of that privilege, many Christians become busy with natural things. They say, "Oh yes, amen. I know the Holy Spirit lives in me," and then walk off and act like He doesn't. They don't give Him any time and attention. They don't spend enough time tuning in to Him through prayer and the Word of God to hear His voice. As a result, they miss out on His leadings.

If you'll learn to be sensitive to the Holy Spirit, He'll help you at the most surprising times. You might just be going about your daily business, doing household chores or driving down the street, and suddenly the Spirit of God will move in you and you'll be enlightened. He'll tell you something you desperately need to know. What a wonderful blessing.

I remember one time specifically when that happened to me, I was driving home in my car. As I turned into our neighborhood, the Holy Spirit moved in my heart and a light went on in my spirit. (Proverbs 20:27 says, *"The spirit of man is the candle of the Lord...."* He gives light to your spirit so you know which way to go.)

"Thou wilt show me the path of life: in thy presence is fulness of joy; at thy right hand there are pleasures for evermore" (Psalm 16:11). *"But the path of the uncompromisingly just*

and righteous is like the light of dawn, that shines more and more—brighter and clearer—until [it reaches its full strength and glory in] the perfect (to-be-prepared) day" (Proverbs 4:18, *The Amplified Bible*).

During the previous weeks, Ken and I had been talking with a builder who wanted to develop a subdivision on some of the ministry property. At the time, the ministry needed money and since we had no immediate plans for that land, selling it seemed a practical thing to do. So we'd been praying about it.

Plans had been made. Papers were being drawn up and, although we hadn't signed anything, the deal was ready to be finalized.

But that day as I was turning into our neighborhood, a light went on in my heart and I received strong direction from the Lord saying, *Don't you do it! Don't you sell that land!*

It was over in a flash. As far as Ken and I were concerned, that settled the matter. We never again considered that housing development. Even though we desperately needed the money at the time, we just cut off negotiations.

Of course, the money we needed came in through other avenues. God provided for us as He always does, and the ministry still owns the land. What's more, I'm sure the Holy Spirit saved us untold trouble by steering us clear of that situation.

The Only Safe Way to Live

The Holy Ghost is no respecter of persons. He didn't give me that guidance because Ken and I are in the ministry. He gave it to me because we followed Proverbs 3:5-6: *"Trust in the Lord with all thine heart; and lean not unto thine own understanding. In all thy ways acknowledge him, and he shall direct thy paths."* We asked Him for His will in the matter and expected Him to reveal it to us.

"I just don't know about that," you may say. "I don't think I have the kind of connection with God that you do."

Yes, you do, if you're born of God. I'm sure of it because the Apostle John wrote a letter to believers and said without qualification:

> **As for you, (the sacred appointment, the unction) the anointing which you received from Him, abides (permanently) in you; [so] then you have no need that any one should instruct you. But just as His anointing teaches you concerning everything, and is true, and is no falsehood, so you must abide...in Him... (1 John 2:27, *The Amplified Bible*).**

If you're a believer, you have the anointing or unction of the Holy Spirit within you. That anointing is there to lead and guide you. If you'll maintain a lifestyle of spending time with God and putting His Word in your heart, then that anointing will talk to you and continually give you the answers and information you need to walk in victory in every area of your life. If you'll live in contact with God, listening for His Spirit and being pliable and quick to change when He speaks (and patient to wait on Him until you hear His voice), He'll keep you out of bad situations. He'll keep you out of court. He'll keep you out of the lawyer's office. He'll keep you out of bad business deals and all kinds of other catastrophes.

If you ignore that anointing, however, and just forge ahead making decisions based strictly on your natural intelligence without praying and seeking God, too often you'll find yourself in more trouble than you can handle.

It's a wonderful thing to be filled with the Holy Ghost! It's a wonderful thing to be able to hear from heaven about your daily life and receive supernatural guidance about what to do.

But you have to cultivate that ability. You can't just spend your time attending ballgames and watching TV, and then run to your pastor for prayer and a word of wisdom when you need it. If you've been doing that, stop it. That is nothing more than spiritual laziness, and it will eventually land you in trouble.

You need to start doing your own praying. You can't depend on another person's faith—even if that other person is your pastor. Your pastor is there to help you and he'll build you up and teach you the Word, but he's not God. As you grow up spiritually, you are able to go to God, pray the prayer of faith and hear from Him yourself.

God didn't give you the Holy Spirit so you could be dependent on someone else. He gave you the Holy Spirit so you could be dependent on *Him!* So build your life in such a way that you can hear from heaven yourself. Draw near to God and He will draw near to you. Learn how to listen to your Counselor.

Granted, that will take time and effort, but it's the only safe way to live. After all, the pastor may have more problems than you do. Your needs might not be top priority on his list. He might forget to pray about them, but you won't! Your problems are more important to you than to anyone else on Earth. So don't expect someone else to solve them for you.

If you're a new Christian, you may have to depend on others for a while until you have time to develop your own faith. But don't be content to remain a spiritual baby. Get busy. Spend time in the Word and in prayer. Study what the Bible has to say about the Holy Spirit within you. Build your faith in Him.

Meditate on all the Holy Spirit has been sent to do for you. He's come not only to teach you, but also to show you things to come. As Christians, we ought not to be in the dark. We ought to know the things that are coming upon the Earth. We ought to be like Noah. When all the world around him was in the dark about what was about to happen, Noah was hearing from God. The Holy Spirit told him what was coming and told him how to plan for it. So when the flood came, Noah wasn't in the dark—he was in the ark!

The Holy Spirit will do the same thing for us if we'll just pay attention to Him. He'll let us know what's ahead so that we can prepare and continue to do what we're called to do, regardless of what happens to the economy or any other natural situation.

What's more, when we face hard situations, He'll be our Strengthener. When we feel ourselves growing weak and starting to slip into fear or doubt, He will speak to us and give us light from the Word that will make us strong again.

The Amplified Bible says He'll also be our Standby. What does that mean? It means He'll be standing by to help you when you need it.

Sometimes you'll be moving through life just fine, and then you hit a challenge that requires something extra. It's like you're climbing up a mountain and you need a push to help you over the top. The Holy Spirit will give you that extra boost. If you will look to Him in faith, He will help you when the pressures of circumstances become too great.

His strength and ability is limitless, so He always has what you need.

Remember this: Everything that Jesus has, all that He is, is made available to you through the Holy Spirit. You have everything when you are filled with Him. But to enjoy His provision, you must spend time with Him. You must live vitally united to Him, maintaining living contact with Him continually.

Learn to commune with the Lord all through the day. Worship Him. Visit with Him. Sing to Him. Listen to Him. Brother Lawrence, a monk from the 1600s, is still a famous Christian today because He learned to "practice the presence of God" even in everyday tasks and mundane chores. He learned how to walk in the spirit and live in the spirit. We can learn how, too, if we will give ourselves to God and let Him be the biggest thing in our lives.

9

Wellsprings and Rivers
Receiving the Fullness of the Holy Spirit

To enjoy the full measure of living contact with God, you must realize that the Bible speaks of two distinct experiences with the Holy Spirit that are available to every believer. The first is the entrance of the Holy Spirit into your spirit that took place the moment you were born again. It was that experience Jesus referred to in John 4 when He spoke to the woman at the well and said:

> **If thou knewest the gift of God, and who it is that saith to thee, Give me to drink; thou wouldest have asked of him, and he would have given thee living water.... Whosoever drinketh of this [natural] water shall thirst again: But whosoever drinketh of the water that I shall give him shall never thirst; but the water that I shall give him shall be in him a well of water springing up into everlasting life (verses 10, 13-14).**

Every person who has made Jesus Christ the Lord of his life has a well of life that flows out by the Holy Spirit inside him. He can sense the prompting of that life, and he can draw on the wellspring of that living water to meet his own personal needs.

Whenever I think of the supernatural well of water springing up into everlasting life, I think of the water well Ken and I have at our prayer cabin in Arkansas. It's a good well. In fact, it's a faith well. I had to believe God for it.

When the workmen first began digging it, they stopped about midway down and said, "Mrs. Copeland, there's no point in our digging any farther, because we know there's no water there." I asked them how they knew, and they told me they had run into a certain kind of soil that indicated the well would be dry.

Since I had found a scripture in the Bible that says, *"Water for him will be sure"* (Isaiah 33:16, *The Amplified Bible)*, I said, "You just go back out there and keep digging." They did and, sure enough, that turned out to be a very good well. Even in dry weather, it doesn't run dry (unless I forget and leave the hose running).

One thing I have noticed about that well, however, is that it seeks a certain level and stays there. It never overflows. It doesn't rush forth like a river to supply the whole county with water. It supplies just what we need and no more.

That's how the well of the newborn spirit is indwelt by the Holy Spirit. It supplies the Water of Life to the individual believer. It helps him with his own life, but it doesn't supply enough power to help anyone else.

Let the Rivers Flow!

Some denominations have taught that the wellspring of the Holy Spirit received at the new birth is all God intends for us to have. But the Bible teaches us that something more is available. John 7:37-39 speaks of that something more, saying:

In the last day, that great day of the feast, Jesus stood and cried, saying, If any man thirst, let him come unto me, and drink. He that believeth on me, as the scripture hath said, out of his belly shall flow rivers of living water. (But this spake he of the Spirit, which they that believe on him should receive: for the Holy Ghost was not yet given; because that Jesus was not yet glorified.)

Notice Jesus didn't mention a well there. He didn't talk about a spring. He talked about rivers! A well just sits there, but a river takes its course wherever it wants to go. A river is powerful. It doesn't just belong to one person—it's there for everyone. It supplies water to multitudes.

God never intended us as believers to have just enough of the Holy Spirit to take care of ourselves personally. It's His will for us to be overflowing with His power. It's His will for us to live in such striking victory that we are living demonstrations to the multitudes that Jesus is alive! He wants rivers of the Spirit flowing through us, so we can cast out devils, speak with new tongues, lay hands on the sick and see them recover. (See Mark 16:17-18.)

In other words, God wants us to receive the Baptism in the Holy Spirit just as the first disciples did, so we can act just like they acted! So we can obey the words of Jesus. *"I assure you, most solemnly I tell you, if anyone steadfastly believes in Me, he will himself be able to do the things that I do; and he will do even greater things than these, because I go to the Father"* (John 14:12, *The Amplified Bible*).

Jesus ascended to the Father so we could receive the Baptism in the Holy Spirit! It's that baptism which was on His mind when, after His death and Resurrection, He left His disciples for the last time. Acts 1 says:

> **And, being assembled together with them, [Jesus] commanded them that they should not depart from Jerusalem, but wait for the promise of the Father, which, saith he, ye have heard of me. For John truly baptized with water; but ye shall be baptized with the Holy Ghost not many days hence.... But ye shall receive power, after that the Holy Ghost is come upon you: and ye shall be witnesses unto me both in Jerusalem, and in all Judaea, and in Samaria, and unto the uttermost part of the earth. And when he had spoken these things, while they beheld, he was taken up; and a cloud received him out of their sight (verses 4-5, 8-9).**

These disciples were already born again. Jesus had already breathed on them after His resurrection and said, *"Receive ye the Holy Ghost"* (John 20:22), so they had the Spirit indwelling them. But that was not enough. Jesus said they needed to have another experience. They needed to be baptized or immersed in that Spirit. They needed power—not just the Spirit within but the Spirit upon. They needed to be anointed with the Holy Ghost and power.

My, what a change occurred when they received the power of the Holy Ghost! This group that had been so weak and confused during the Crucifixion and afraid that the Jews would come after them, came bursting out of the upper room with boldness and power, speaking with tongues as the Spirit gave them utterance.

Among them was Peter, who had just a few weeks earlier been so afraid of persecution that he denied even knowing Jesus. Yet once baptized in the Holy Spirit, he had the spiritual boldness to point at the same people he had once feared and say:

> **Ye men of Israel, hear these words; Jesus of Nazareth, a man approved of God among you by miracles and wonders and signs, which God did by him in the midst of you, as ye yourselves also know: Him, being delivered by the determinate counsel and foreknowledge of God, ye have taken, and by wicked hands have crucified and slain: Whom God hath raised up.... Repent, and be baptized every one of you in the name of Jesus Christ for the remission of sins, and ye shall receive the gift of the Holy Ghost. For the promise is unto you, and to your children, and to all that are afar off, even as many as the Lord our God shall call (Acts 2:22-24, 38-39).**

The Baptism in the Holy Spirit Is for All

Some people have said the Baptism in the Holy Spirit was just for those first disciples. But that's not what Peter said. He said, it's for *all*—for you and your children. *"The promise [of the Holy Ghost] is unto you, and to your children, and to all that are afar off, even as many as the Lord our God shall call"* (Acts 2:39). That means you and me. If you'll read through the book of Acts, you'll see that confirmed repeatedly. Again and again, you'll see the new believers in the early Church receiving the Baptism in the Holy Spirit after they were born again. In the Scripture it's obviously a separate and distinct experience made available to those who have been born again.

In Acts 8, for example, Philip went to Samaria and preached the gospel to the people there. Many were born again and baptized in water. The Samaritans, however, did not automatically receive the Baptism in the Holy Spirit when they were born again. They received it at a later time.

> **When the apostles which were at Jerusalem heard that Samaria had received the word of God, they sent unto them Peter and John: Who, when they were come down, prayed for them, that they might receive the Holy Ghost: (For as yet he was fallen upon none of them: only they were baptized in the name of the Lord Jesus.) Then they laid their hands on them, and they received the Holy Ghost (verses 14-17).**

We find a similar occurrence recorded in Acts 19 when Paul, during his missionary travels, came upon some disciples of John the Baptist in Ephesus:

> **[Paul] said unto them, Have ye received the Holy Ghost since ye believed? And they said unto him, We have not so much as heard whether there be any Holy Ghost. And he said unto them, Unto what then were ye**

baptized? And they said, Unto John's baptism. Then said Paul, John verily baptized with the baptism of repentance, saying unto the people, that they should believe on him which should come after him, that is, on Christ Jesus. When they heard this, they were baptized in the name of the Lord Jesus. And when Paul had laid his hands upon them, the Holy Ghost came on them; and they spake with tongues, and prophesied (verses 2-6).

Notice once again the two separate experiences. These people first believed on Jesus and were baptized in water in His Name (the new birth). Then Paul laid hands on them and they received the Baptism in the Holy Spirit.

The Value of Praying in Tongues

Although these two experiences do not always occur at the same time, they can, and it is most wonderful when they do. In Acts 10 when the gospel was first preached by Peter to the gentiles, that is what happened. Although Peter did not lay hands on these people, they clearly received both the new birth and the Baptism in the Holy Spirit as Peter was preaching to them of Jesus:

While Peter yet spake these words, the Holy Ghost fell on all them which heard the word. And they of the circumcision which believed were astonished, as many as came with Peter, because that on the Gentiles also was poured out the gift of the Holy Ghost. For they heard them speak with tongues, and magnify God.

Then answered Peter, Can any man forbid water, that these should not be baptized, which have received the Holy Ghost as well as we? (verses 44-47).

It is important to note that in this instance, as in those recorded in Acts 2, 8 and 19, which we have already discussed, it is either stated outright or clearly implied that all those who received the Baptism in the Holy Spirit gave indication of their experience by speaking in tongues. The same is true today. Speaking in tongues is the outward evidence of the Baptism in the Holy Spirit.

Some Christians are uncomfortable with that. "Do I have to speak in tongues?" they ask.

No, you don't *have* to...you *get* to! Speaking in tongues is not some spiritual badge of honor. It is an indispensable tool God has given you to help you live a victorious and powerful life. It is a tool you desperately need.

As believers still living in natural bodies, you and I need to be able to pray in tongues because we have weaknesses. Our understanding of spiritual things is limited. We don't yet know all we need to know. That lack of knowledge would constantly hinder our ability to pray according to the will of God if it weren't for the provision God has made that enables us to overcome it. Romans 8 describes that provision:

So too the (Holy) Spirit comes to our aid and bears us up in our weakness; for we do not know what prayer to offer nor how to offer it worthily as we ought, but the Spirit Himself goes to meet our supplication and pleads in our behalf with unspeakable yearnings and groanings too deep for utterance. And He Who searches

**the hearts of men knows what is in the mind of the
(Holy) Spirit—what His intent is—because the Spirit
intercedes and pleads [before God] in behalf of the
saints according to and in harmony with God's will
(verses 26-27, *The Amplified Bible*).**

First Corinthians 14:2 further describes this process, saying, *"For he that speaketh in an unknown tongue speaketh not
unto men, but unto God: for no man understandeth him;
howbeit in the spirit he speaketh mysteries."*

You and I need to be praying about what will happen to us
tomorrow. We need to be praying about God's plan for us and
our families five years from now. We need to be praying out
the plan of God for this Earth. But many times we don't know
those things. They are mysteries to us. What can we do? Pray
in tongues!

Praying in tongues or in the Spirit enables you to pray the
perfect will of God for your life. It allows you to step out of the
realm of the flesh and into the realm of the spirit, so that no
matter how weak or ignorant you may be in the natural, you
can pray exactly as you need to pray as the Spirit gives
you utterance.

Sometimes you will have an insight, a word, an interpreta-
tion of what you are praying in the Spirit. Say to the Lord,
"The things I know not, teach me, and the things I see not,
show me." You'll begin to receive revelation on things you've
never before understood. That's what you need, revelation
from God! That's what we all need. The result of praying in
tongues might come to you later as "a knowing"—you'll just
know something. You'll have a word of knowledge from the
Spirit of God (1 Corinthians 12:8). God has things that are so

far better for us than what we've seen that we can't even figure them out. But if we'll pray in the Spirit, we'll reach into that area out beyond our knowledge and expectation, *"above all that we ask or think"* (Ephesians 3:20).

Is it any wonder that speaking in tongues has undergone such persecution? The devil hates it! He knows it's the only way believers can pray beyond what they know and into the limitless possibilities of the Spirit of God.

He understands (even if we don't) that even baby Christians, newly reborn, can pray in tongues, receive the mind of the Spirit and start growing fast. That's the way the church at Jerusalem grew in the early days. That's all they had. They couldn't take their New Testaments and read Paul's letter to the Ephesians or the Epistles of John. They just had to use the ability and understanding the Holy Spirit had given them. And when they did, they turned the whole world upside down. Study the entire chapter of 1 Corinthians 14 concerning this.

Build Yourself Up by Praying

You and I can have the spiritual strength it takes to turn our world upside down for Jesus too, if we'll just commit ourselves to spend time each day praying in the Spirit. For it will not only enlighten us, it will enable us to overcome the weakness of our flesh.

Our flesh and blood bodies haven't been reborn like our spirit has. If we don't take control of them, they will take us from one failure to another. So what we must do is build up our spirit, strengthen it to the point that it can dominate, or rule over, our flesh.

Praying in tongues helps us do that. As Jude 20 says, *"But you, beloved, build yourselves up [founded] on your most holy faith—make progress, rise like an edifice higher and higher—praying in the Holy Spirit" (The Amplified Bible).*

Praying in tongues will pump you up like a spiritual body builder. It will enable you to walk in the power of the Spirit instead of the weakness of the flesh.

Prayer of any kind, whether it's with the Spirit or with the understanding, is an absolute necessity if you want to be spiritually strong and ready in times of crisis.

In Luke 21:36, Jesus says, *"Watch ye therefore, and pray always, that ye may be accounted worthy,"* or as *The Amplified Bible* says, *"that you may have the full strength and ability...to escape all these things...that will take place."*

If you want to have the strength and ability to come through troubled times in triumph, you'd better spend some time in prayer. That's what Jesus urged Peter and the other disciples to do in the Garden of Gethsemane. He knew they were about to face one of the toughest times of their lives. He said, *"Watch ye and pray, lest ye enter into temptation. The spirit truly is ready, but the flesh is weak"* (Mark 14:38).

Instead of obeying Jesus' admonition to pray, the Scripture tells us the disciples went to sleep. In Peter's life in particular, we can see the result. When temptation came, he entered into it and denied the Lord.

You might as well face it. Temptation will come to you as long as you live in a flesh body. So you'd better stay prayed up! Tests will come as long as we live in the flesh, but we can pass them if we'll obey our spirit and not our flesh. After all, it is an open book test!

I remember when God first began to speak to me about the importance of praying in the Spirit. I'd been asking Him to show me how to quit living my life so much on the natural, circumstantial level and start walking in the spirit.

I'd been committed to the Word for years at that time. I regularly spent much time reading and meditating on it—and that alone had already revolutionized my life. But I knew there was still something lacking.

What God showed me was that I needed to add to the Word by praying more, and He spoke to me specifically about praying in other tongues. Today I can understand why. When I began to pray more in tongues, I began to give my spirit more outflow. I gave vent to it. I became spiritually stronger. It completely changed me. I am so different now than I was before and still changing!

Giving vent to your spirit is the way you walk in the spirit, just like giving vent to your flesh is the way you walk in the flesh. The more I released my spirit through tongues, the more my spirit began to take charge. I found it worked just as the Bible says, if you *"walk in the spirit...ye shall not fulfil the lust of the flesh"* (Galatians 5:16). I found it easier to hear and obey my spirit indwelt by the Holy Spirit.

Isn't that simple? The devil has tried to hide the simplicity of it from us because he knows if we ever start doing it, he'll have no place left. He's limited. He can't touch your reborn spirit. The only thing he has to work on is your flesh. Once you learn what brings the flesh under dominion, once you learn that praying in the Spirit applies spirit to flesh and causes the flesh to obey God the way it should, the devil won't be able to obtain a foothold in your life at all! Rivers of the Spirit start flowing out of you to change things supernaturally!

How to Receive the Baptism in the Holy Spirit

If you never have received the Baptism in the Holy Spirit, if you never have prayed in other tongues, I urge you not to let one more day go by without doing so. It isn't difficult. The only condition you must meet to qualify for it is that of making Jesus Christ the Lord of your life. You must be born again.

Once you have met that condition, the Baptism in the Holy Spirit is yours for the asking. You don't have to be afraid that you won't receive it, or that you will receive some evil counterfeit, for Jesus said:

> **Every one that asketh receiveth; and he that seeketh findeth; and to him that knocketh it shall be opened. If a son shall ask bread of any of you that is a father, will he give him a stone? or if he ask a fish, will he for a fish give him a serpent? Or if he shall ask an egg, will he offer him a scorpion? If ye then, being evil, know how to give good gifts unto your children: how much more shall your heavenly Father give the Holy Spirit to them that ask him? (Luke 11:10-13).**

To receive the Baptism in the Holy Spirit, all you must do is ask and in simple faith receive. Simply lift your heart to God and say:

> **Father, I come to You now in the Name of Jesus. I have received Him as my Savior and the Lord of my life and I stand before You now, cleansed by the precious Blood He shed for me. Lord, You said in Your Word that the promise of the Holy Spirit is for me. So in faith I take**

You at Your Word. I ask You to baptize me and fill me to overflowing with Your own precious Spirit. Thank You, Lord, for fulfilling Your promise to me. I fully expect now for the Holy Spirit to take hold together with me as I pray and give me utterance in other tongues.

After you have prayed, give expression to your faith by lifting your heartfelt thanks and praises to God. But instead of speaking in your own language, allow the language of the Spirit to flow from within you.

Do not wait for the Holy Spirit to make you speak, because He will not do so. Nowhere does the Bible teach that the Holy Spirit does the speaking. It is the believers themselves who speak. The Holy Ghost simply cooperates with us, supplying us the language as we begin to speak out by faith.

Don't be concerned with what the words sound like to you. In fact, don't concentrate on the words at all. Just focus your attention on the Lord. Think about how much you love Him. Think about how wonderful and loving and kind He is. Think about the matchless privilege of having a living connection with Him. As you do, just rejoice and trust Him, and although you may feel you are stuttering or stumbling at first, relax in the confidence that God will perfect your praise (Matthew 21:16).

I'll warn you in advance, the devil will probably try to harass you. He may tell you you're silly to speak words you don't understand. If that doesn't work, he may tell you you're *not smart enough* to speak words you don't understand. When he does, just remember this: Every born-again believer from the least to the greatest can pray in tongues. You don't have to be smart to do it. But without a doubt, if you'll shove aside those devilish doubts and persist, if you'll make living contact with God by praying in tongues every day, it will eventually prove to be one of the smartest things you ever did.

Now you can say, according to 1 John 4:

I do not believe every spirit, but test the spirits, whether they are of God; because many false prophets have gone out into the world.

By this I know the Spirit of God: Every spirit that confesses that Jesus Christ has come in the flesh is of God, and every spirit that does not confess that Jesus Christ has come in the flesh is not of God. And this is the spirit of the Antichrist, which I have heard was coming, and is now already in the world.

I am of God and have overcome them, because He who is in me is greater than he who is in the world. They are of the world. Therefore they speak as of the world, and the world hears them. I am of God. He who knows God hears me; he who is not of God does not hear me. By this I know the spirit of truth and the spirit of error.

I love others, for love is of God, and everyone who loves is born of God and knows God. He who does not love does not know God, for God is love. In this the love of God was manifested toward me, that God sent His only begotten Son into the world, that I might live through Him. In this is love, not that I loved God, but that He loved me and sent His Son to be the propitiation for my sins. If God so loved me, I also ought to love others.

No one has seen God at any time. If I love others, God abides in me, and His love has been perfected in

me. By this I know that I abide in Him, and He in me, because He has given me of His Spirit.

And I have seen and testify that the Father has sent the Son as Savior of the world. Whoever confesses that Jesus is the Son of God, God abides in him, and he in God. And I have known and believed the love that God has for me. God is love, and he who abides in love abides in God, and God in him.

Love has been perfected in me in this: that I may have boldness in the day of judgment; because as He is, so am I in this world. There is no fear in love; but perfect love casts out fear, because fear involves torment. But he who fears has not been made perfect in love. I love Him because He first loved me.

If someone says, "I love God," and hates his brother, he is a liar; for he who does not love his brother whom he has seen, how can he love God whom he has not seen? And this commandment I have from Him: that he who loves God must love his brother also.

Hallelujah!

10

Staying Hooked Up to Heaven

Perhaps the greatest challenge we face as Spirit-filled believers is that of learning to accurately distinguish the voice of the Holy Spirit. It is not an easy task because when we begin, we are such carnal thinkers. But it is definitely worthwhile, because if we are to abide in the Lord, to maintain a living connection with Him, we must be able to hear and obey the leadings of His Spirit. God has always expected His people to do that. If you'll read the Old Testament, you'll see that God told Israel not only to obey His written Word, but also to obey His voice (Jeremiah 7:23). He wanted them to know His will in specific situations.

When the army of Israel invaded Jericho, they had to hear God's voice. Where else would they have acquired the strange battle plan they used? It wasn't written in the law of Moses. And certainly, no human being would suggest a seven-day march around a city as the most effective form of invasion!

No, that was God's plan. He told it to Joshua and when Joshua followed it, there was victory. For us to walk in victory today, we must do the same thing Joshua did. We must not only obey the written Word, we must also be able to hear and obey God's instructions to us about the choices and decisions we face each day.

Say, for example, you are offered a job in another city. Naturally speaking, it may seem to be a great opportunity. It might involve an increase in pay or a promotion. But to be sure what to do, you need guidance from the Lord.

You can open the Bible and receive some general instructions that may help you. But the written Word of God will not tell you whether to take that job or not. You won't find a chapter and verse that says, "Yes, that's a good move. Go to Chicago next May and take the job there. That's God's will for you."

To find out what choice is right in such situations, you must be able to discern the voice or the promptings of the Holy Spirit. You must be sensitive to His leadings in your heart.

How do you cultivate that kind of discernment and sensitivity? In several ways.

The first two, which we've already addressed at length, are to spend time praying (both in your own language and in other tongues) daily and meditating on the written Word of God. The more familiar you are with God's voice as it comes through the written Word, the more easily you'll be able to recognize His voice in your own heart. Through the written Word, your mind becomes renewed to accept God's ways as the right thing to do.

Another major key to developing and maintaining spiritual sensitivity is to stay hooked up to the realm of the spirit throughout the day. Don't just have your daily time in prayer and the Word, and then barrel through the rest of your day, forgetting all about God. Stay tuned in to Him. Think of God often; give Him praise; pray in tongues on and off throughout the day. Carry around a pocket New Testament and take a "Word break" instead of a coffee break.

Keep yourself in such a state throughout the day that you're available to God. Whatever your job is, whether you're a business person sitting at a desk or a homemaker buying groceries and cleaning the house, maintain an awareness and living contact with God so that at any moment, if He needs to let you know something, He can reach you.

It is possible to keep your mind so stayed on God that no matter what you come up against, you're just one moment away from hearing from the Holy Spirit. If you'll maintain your union with God throughout the day by making Him the number one priority and continually walking in love, you can stay hooked up to heaven 24 hours a day. You can rest in the assurance that you have all of heaven's resources backing you and that the Holy Ghost is constantly with you, ready to talk to you about anything you need to know.

You must remember, however, that the Holy Spirit is a gentleman. He won't force Himself on you. If you want Him to be active in your life, you must give Him place. You must be constantly looking to Him for guidance, instead of managing your life according to your own fleshly plans and ideas.

I have a friend who operates in a great, supernatural ministry. He prayed for years that the Spirit of God would manifest Himself in his meetings. Finally, one day the Lord answered him and said, *You don't give Me any opportunity!* In other words, my friend had his agenda, and he was not leaving any time or space for the Spirit of God to move.

We've all done that at times. In our meetings and our churches, we have such a habit of doing certain things—of singing a set number of songs, receiving the offering at a particular time and preaching a certain way—that we shut out the Holy Spirit. When my friend realized that's what he was doing, he changed some things.

We need to do the same, not just in our corporate services, but in our individual lives as well. We need to slow down a little and invite the Holy Spirit to interrupt our neat, little plans if He wants. If we don't make place for Him, He will not push His way in.

He won't come in while you're sitting on the couch watching television, slap the remote out of your hand and say, "Shut that thing off! I have something to tell you and I can't get a word in edgewise."

No, He just doesn't do that. You have to make place for Him. He will not take over your life. He will wait for you to draw near to Him, and when you do, He'll draw near to you.

So purpose to draw near to Him throughout your day. When you're in your car, for instance, instead of listening to talk radio, put in a teaching tape and listen to the Word of God. When you're dressing for work, instead of listening to secular music, spend that time singing songs to the Lord and praising Him.

Little things like that can make a great difference in your day. I know that from experience. Some mornings when I wake up, I'd rather do almost anything than go into the television studio and tape the daily broadcast. But during the 15-minute drive from our house to the studio, I'll play a praise tape or just begin to worship God. By the time I arrive at the studio, I will be singing and praising God. My heart will be lifted and strong and I'll be ready to preach!

Learn to take advantage of such times throughout your day. Take a few minutes here and there to keep yourself strong and built up in the Lord.

Be Available

If you'll be faithful to maintain that kind of sensitivity and living contact with the Holy Spirit, you'll be amazed at what God can do for you and through you. He'll enable you to do greater things than you ever imagined. He'll enable you to live like an overcomer and be a blessing to many, many people.

You may not think you have the ability to do anything of consequence. But that doesn't bother God. He isn't looking for ability. He is looking for availability! All He needs is faithfulness.

It would be wonderful, I suppose, to have great natural talent. But when you hook up with God, it doesn't really matter whether you're talented or not. God has all the talent and ability He needs. He doesn't necessarily search out a shining star at some major university and say, "Look at that guy! He is such a wonderful speaker. I think he would make Me a good preacher."

That rarely ever happens. God is much more likely to seek out someone like Oral Roberts. When God called him, he was a 17-year-old boy who stuttered so badly he could hardly say his own name. He was weak and sick, dying of tuberculosis. But he was available. So God cured him of stuttering, healed his disease and made him one of the most outstanding healing evangelists of all time.

If you'll maintain living contact with God, it won't matter what you are in the natural. You may be poor or uneducated. You may be the biggest failure on your block. But those things just make you a prime candidate for the calling of God. As the Apostle Paul wrote:

> **The foolishness of God is wiser than men; and the weakness of God is stronger than men. For ye see your calling, brethren, how that not many wise men after the flesh, not many mighty, not many noble, are called: But God hath chosen the foolish things of the world to confound the wise; and God hath chosen the weak things of the world to confound the things which are mighty; And base things of the world, and things which are despised, hath God chosen, yea, and things which are not, to bring to nought things that are: That no flesh should glory in his presence.**
>
> **But of him are ye in Christ Jesus, who of God is made unto us wisdom, and righteousness, and sanctification, and redemption: That, according as it is written, He that glorieth, let him glory in the Lord (1 Corinthians 1:25-31).**

The new birth is the great equalizer. It takes you out of your natural station in life (whether it be low or high) and puts you in the Anointed Jesus and His Anointing. It makes available to you the wisdom and ability of God Himself. As you make yourself available to Him, He'll cause that ability to flow through you by anointing you to do whatever He wants you to do.

It thrills me to know that I don't have to be special to be used by God. I just have to be faithful. I just have to yield myself to Him and stay in living contact with Him. To me, that's a tremendous encouragement.

Cultivate an Attitude of Dependency

Actually, I think one of the things that has helped me most has been my awareness of my own natural inadequacy. From the moment God called Ken and me into ministry, I have been aware that I was in over my head. I knew I did not have the ability in the natural to do what God was telling us to do.

Some people feel self-sufficient. They think they are smart enough or talented enough to do things on their own. And though they may have some good results, they'll never see the kinds of supernatural results they would if they were dependent on God.

For me, however, self-sufficiency isn't much of a temptation. In the ministry, everything you have to do is impossible with men, so I have to start every day dependent on the Holy Spirit. I rarely do anything in the mornings before I pray. I don't even drink a cup of coffee in the morning before I have my prayer time. I like to make a connection with God first thing in the morning. I like to talk to Him about the things I'm facing that day. If I have a business meeting, I want to know what He has to say about the issues we'll be discussing at that meeting. I don't want to go in there and be dependent on natural knowledge. If I'm ministering, I have to be anointed by His Spirit, or I might as well stay home.

As far as I'm concerned, I can't afford to step out of my house before I've spent time with God.

Actually, the same is true for you. Even if you aren't in the fivefold ministry, as a believer you're called to do impossible things. You're called to lay hands on the sick, for example, and deliver the healing power of God. I don't care how smart and talented you are, you can't do that without depending on the Holy Spirit.

If you're ever tempted to think you can, remember this: Even Jesus had to depend on the Holy Spirit to carry out His ministry. Although He was the sinless Son of God from the moment He was born, He never did a single miracle until the Holy Spirit came upon Him.

What's more, even after His baptism in the Holy Spirit, Jesus said, *"I am able to do nothing from Myself—independently, of My own accord—but as I am taught by God and as I get His orders..."* (John 5:30, *The Amplified Bible*). He could only live and minister in victory by living in total dependence on God.

Jesus walked out His earth life just the way you and I are called to walk out our earth life. He would continually abide in the Father and His Words, be obedient and hear from heaven what to do. Jesus didn't live unto Himself. He lived every moment hearing from the Father and obeying Him.

If you'll look at Jesus' ministry, you'll find His prayer life was amazing. He would minister to people all day long, and then He would spend all night long alone with God. Why did He do that? Because He was completely dependent on God. Jesus knew He had to receive direction and instructions from the Holy Spirit if He was to do what God had called Him to do.

If that was true for Jesus, it is true for you too! So follow His example and cultivate an attitude of dependency on the Holy Spirit. Ask the Holy Spirit to help you develop such a habit of dependence on Him that it would be unusual for you to go more than 15 or 20 minutes without talking to Him and looking to Him for assistance.

Heed the instructions in Colossians 2 and *"just as you trusted Christ [the Anointed One and His Anointing] to save you, trust him, too, for each day's problems; live in vital union with him"* (verse 6, *The Living Bible).* In other words, depend on Him to help you through the things that you face in your life. Become so Holy Ghost-minded that the first thing you think about when a pain or symptom of sickness tries to attach itself to your body is not your doctor—it's the Word of God and the power of His Spirit. Become so dependent on Him that when you encounter financial trouble, you don't go running to your banker first...you go running to Him.

The more you depend on the Holy Spirit, the more you will open the door for Him to be active in your life. It's your dependency on Him that clears the way for Him to move. So don't try to make decisions by yourself. You don't know the future. Lean on the Holy Spirit. He knows what's ahead.

Every day, acknowledge your dependency on Him. Say something like this:

Lord, I am so grateful for the Holy Spirit Who lives in me and teaches me the things I need to know. I'm so grateful He is dwelling in me to be my Guide in every situation and to lead me into all truth. I'm totally dependent upon You, Lord. I'm just like a little child. I don't know whether to come in or go out unless You show me what to do. And I'm glad to be that way because I love You and trust You with my whole heart.

Help me today to walk in intimacy with You all day long. Teach me to live and walk in the spirit, not just when I'm in trouble, but every moment in union and communion with You.

I trust in the Lord with all my heart, and lean not to my own understanding. I acknowledge You in all my ways, and You shall direct my path according to Your

Word. In Jesus' Name, I expect to receive guidance today. Thank You, Father, for helping me and directing me (Proverbs 3:5-6).

11

Expect to Be Led by the Spirit

Inevitably when I refer to hearing from the Spirit of God, someone will say, "I can't hear God's voice! He just doesn't speak to me like He speaks to you."

If that is the case with you, there are several possible reasons for it. You may be hindered because you haven't been spending enough time with Him to be sensitive to His voice.

You may also be blocking your ability to hear with your own unbelief. Jesus said plainly, *"My sheep hear my voice"* (John 10:27). Therefore, if you are a born-again child of God, you not only *can* but *should* expect to hear God speaking to you. To say you cannot hear Him is to doubt the words of Jesus Himself, so don't do it. Instead, use your words to express your faith. Say, "I can hear from God! I know I can because Jesus said so! His sheep know His voice." If you'll begin to believe and confess the scriptures about being led by the Lord, you'll begin to discern His leadership and distinguish His guidance.

It's likely that you are already hearing from God, but you aren't recognizing it because you are listening for the wrong thing. Often people expect God to speak to them forcefully. They are looking for a burning bush or listening for an audible voice. But normally God speaks to us in less dramatic ways.

His leadings are usually very subtle. They rise up in your heart like holy suggestions. When you sense those "suggestions," you may even wonder, *Was that me, Lord, or was that You?* That's because God doesn't normally inject thoughts directly into your mind from the outside. Instead, He impresses or enlightens your spirit, and your spirit translates that impression into a thought. So when you receive it, it sounds like you. It *was* you! It was your spirit being influenced by the Spirit of God within you.

Such Holy Spirit impressions hardly ever come in and overwhelm you. They come most often in the form of an inward witness or a quiet inner prompting—a knowing—you just suddenly know something you did not know before. Romans 8 gives us an example of how that inner witness works. There the Apostle Paul says, *"The Spirit itself [or Himself] beareth witness with our spirit, that we are the children of God"* (verse 16).

If I were to ask you if you knew you were one of God's children, no doubt you'd answer with a quick, sure "Yes!" But what would you say if I were to ask you how you knew that?

You might answer, "I don't know how I know. I just know!"

What you would actually be saying to me is that the Holy Spirit within you bears witness, or gives assurance to your own spirit, and lets you know that you indeed belong to God.

The inward witness, or promptings of the Spirit, work much that same way in the other affairs of life. You might be going about your day just doing your normal activities and suddenly you'll think, *I need to call Aunt Sally.* You may dismiss the thought at first because you're busy doing other things, but then it recurs. *I need to call Aunt Sally,* you'll think again.

Then you may notice that even though calling Aunt Sally wasn't on your agenda for today, it just seems like a good thing to do right now. So you pick up the phone and dial her number. Very likely, you'll find out that Aunt Sally was discouraged or in need, and your call came just at the right time. Why? Because you yielded to the prompting of the Holy Spirit.

If you will learn to live each day always listening to your heart for that inner witness, constantly expecting to be prompted by the Spirit of God, you'll find yourself doing things like that quite often. Sometimes you won't even realize you're hearing from heaven. You'll just think you had a good idea, but later you'll see that you were responding to the Holy Spirit.

I know of one man, for example, who was living in Oakland, California, and working in San Francisco a few years ago when they had a major earthquake there. He was sitting in his office just a few hours before that quake, when suddenly he had the thought that he should leave work early, so he could avoid the traffic that would be on the roads that evening due to the World Series, which was being held nearby.

It seemed like a purely natural thought at the time, but it seemed good to him (in other words, his heart bore witness with it), so he walked to his car early and drove home. Just a few hours later, at the time he normally would have been driving home, the very freeway he used collapsed in the earthquake.

That goes to show you that staying in living contact with God can save your life!

A Sensitivity You Maintain

If you want to have those kinds of experiences, you will have to learn how to listen to your heart as you go about your day. You will have to learn how to hear the still, small voice on the inside of you—in spite of the bustle and noise on the outside of you!

To do that requires diligence and commitment. It takes a commitment to put God first place in your life every single day. It takes a determination to spend daily time in the Word and in prayer no matter what!

Why is that time so important? Because hearing from God is not as much a skill you learn as it is a sensitivity you maintain. You can be full of knowledge about how to hear God's voice. You may have heard it thousands of times before. But if you want to hear it today, you must be in living contact with Him today. You must maintain fellowship with Him on a continual basis.

It's not enough just to go to church on Sunday. You have to stay in touch with God all the time. With the help of the Holy Spirit, you have to rid your life of things you know are displeasing to God, so your communion with Him won't be hindered. You must be full of the Word of God so that your faith will be strong and your spirit will be receptive to His directions. You must be constantly looking to and listening for Him so that when He speaks, you can hear Him. Otherwise, you'll miss out on those gentle promptings He gives you. You'll be so occupied with your own plans and activities that you won't pay attention to the witness of the Holy Spirit inside.

When you do sense a leading of the Spirit, when you do begin to discern His voice, it's important to obey the instructions in

Hebrews 3:15. *"Today if ye will hear his voice, harden not your [heart]...."* That means don't resist the promptings of the Spirit.

If you sense He is directing you to do something and you decide, consciously or unconsciously, *No, I don't want to do that. I think I'll go another way,* you've just hardened your heart. Most of the time, that's how we miss the will of God. We're not trying to be rebellious. It's just that in one situation or another, we don't follow the leading in our spirit. Our natural mind tells us the reasons why we shouldn't obey that prompting. So we don't.

Let me tell you something. If you insist on being ruled by your natural reasoning and human intellect, the Spirit of God won't be able to get much over to you. Even when He does, you'll end up talking yourself out of it because, quite often, what God tells you to do won't make sense to your mind.

Once when I first began learning to hear the voice of God, I was standing on the front row during the altar call of one of Ken's meetings. He had given the invitation and quite a few people had come to the front of the auditorium. Among them was a young girl about 15 years old. When she walked up there, I sensed an urging in my spirit. *Go up and put your arms around her and love her.*

Was that You, Lord? I asked silently, *or was that me?* I wasn't sure, so I just stood there. Then that impression came back again. *Go up and put your arms around that girl and love her.*

Still, I wasn't sure. Then I began to think of reasons why I shouldn't do it. *I don't want to go up there in front of all those people...I've never done anything like that before...and anyway, I don't even know this girl.* That's the danger of not moving when the Lord tells us to move. We begin to reason, which is the worst thing we can do where walking in the spirit is concerned.

But since I had asked God to teach me how to follow Him, He didn't give up on me. As I stood there trying to remain sensitive to God, I heard Ken say, "Gloria, come up here and put your arm around this girl and just love her." Clearly, God was telling me, *Yes! That was My Spirit!*

Later when I thought about it, I realized it wouldn't have made much difference if I'd obeyed that prompting and been wrong. It wasn't a matter of life and death. It was just a matter of being embarrassed.

That's usually how it is. God won't ask you to part the Red Sea the first day you start learning to hear His voice. He won't tell you to risk your life. He's a master teacher. He knows how to start where you are and deal with you perfectly.

But to obey Him you have to become like a little child. You have to be simple enough to just trust Him and do whatever He tells you to do. Jesus said in Matthew 18:4, *"Whosoever therefore shall humble himself as this little child, the same is greatest in the kingdom of heaven."* If you want to be spiritually great, you have to stop worrying about your image. You have to stop being concerned about looking foolish and caring more about how you look to people than you do about how you look to God.

You must be willing to humble yourself under the mighty hand of God and do whatever He says, even if you think it will make you look silly. And you might as well know right now, some of His instructions will make you look silly to worldly people because they don't understand God's ways.

God told Isaiah, for example, to go naked and barefoot for three years. (He really did! You can read about it in Isaiah 20. *The Amplified Bible* says *"stripped to his loincloth."*) Don't you know Isaiah looked strange to the people around him? But

God said it was a sign and a wonder. Now, I have no under-standing of that, but it serves to remind me that God's ways are very different from our ways.

I can tell you, I didn't go very far in following the Holy Spirit until I said, "Lord, I don't care what I look like to others. If You tell me to do something, I'll do it."

Once you make that decision, obeying God will become much simpler. When you decide you'd rather look ridiculous than risk being disobedient, you're on the verge of an enor-mous breakthrough, because as you follow His promptings, they grow clearer in your spirit.

Stop Wishing and Start Expecting

If you're like me, once you begin identifying the leading of the Spirit, you'll realize you've heard from God in many instances when you didn't even know it. You obeyed the prompting of the Spirit, but because you were expecting something stronger and bolder, you didn't recognize that prompting or unction as a leading of God.

It will probably dawn on you that God has been speaking to you since the day you were born again. He wasn't speaking to you in a way that you could hear with your natural ears. He was speaking to you by enlightening your spirit.

I remember one time in particular when God was very clearly leading me, but I had no idea He was doing it. It was years ago when Ken and I were in Hawaii preaching. The morn-ing we were scheduled to leave, I woke up with a strong desire for a macadamia nut waffle. (The Holy Spirit would never use a macadamia nut waffle to lead Ken, because he doesn't eat things like that. I do, however, so it worked very well for me.)

Of course, I didn't know that hunger was of the Lord. I just thought, *A waffle sounds like a great idea!* So I rushed around and told Ken and the children that I'd go down to the restaurant and find a table. They could meet me there, and we'd eat breakfast before we headed for the airport.

When I entered the restaurant, there were two lines. One was for people who wanted tables outside and the other was for people who wanted to eat inside. I almost always liked to eat outside, but that day I thought, *Well, we'll just eat inside today because we're in a hurry and that line is shorter.*

Then an odd thing happened. Just when it came my turn to be seated, a man stepped right in front of me and took the table that should have been mine. When the hostess came back for me, she led me to a table that was all the way in the back of this large restaurant. At first, I sat down on one side of the table. Then because I wanted to be able to see Ken and the kids when they came in, I moved to the other side of the table.

The chair I chose was right next to another lady who was there eating breakfast. I couldn't have been any closer to her without sitting in her lap. She was right beside me.

As I sat down, she burst into tears. Then she came over to me, put something in my hand and said, "The Lord told me yesterday to give you this ring."

When I saw her tears, I thought perhaps she really didn't want to give it. So I suggested she wait a while and pray about it some more.

"Oh, no!" she said. "I'm not crying because I don't want you to have it. I'm crying because I'm happy. You see, I'm new at learning to hear from God, and yesterday I thought the Lord told me to give this ring to you. I said, 'Lord, if it's really You telling me this, cause Gloria to sit next to me at breakfast in the morning.'"

Obviously the Lord had been leading me through all the choices I had made that morning because I not only sat next to her, I nearly sat on top of her.

That ring was such a blessing to me! It was very unusual. It was a diamond and emerald ring with a setting that constantly spun around and around. During that particular meeting, I had received the revelation of the hundredfold return coming to us in this life, and every time I looked at that ring, it reminded me that my hundredfold return was constantly working, coming to me in this life (Mark 10:30).

If you're sitting there right now wishing things like that would happen to you, stop wishing and start expecting. Then step out and obey the promptings you receive. (I had given a diamond ring away that week because I was prompted to do it.)

Don't be afraid of making a mistake. You have the protection of knowing that the Holy Spirit will never lead you contrary to God's written Word. So don't let that fear hold you back anymore. Keep your spirit in communion with the Holy Spirit, and begin to trust in His ability to lead and guide you.

He can't do anything for you until you trust Him. Just as Jesus couldn't fulfill His ministry as Savior in your life until you trusted Him to save you, the Holy Spirit can't fulfill His role as Comforter, Standby, Helper and Teacher in your life until you depend on Him to do those things. He is waiting on you!

Don't keep Him waiting any longer. Develop a lifestyle of hearing from the Spirit of God by maintaining your fellowship with Him and daring to believe He will lead you. Yes, even you!

12

Guard Your Heart

If I had to capture the secret of staying in living contact with God, of abiding constantly in Him and His blessings, if I had to give you the key to it all in a single phrase, I believe it would be this: *Keep your heart.*

Everything in your life begins in your heart. Your future is literally stored up in your heart. As Jesus said, *"A good man out of the good treasure of the heart bringeth forth good things: and an evil man out of the evil treasure bringeth forth evil things"* (Matthew 12:35).

What you will have in your life tomorrow will be determined by what is in your heart today. If you allow your heart to be filled with cares and anxieties of living, to be crowded with worries and thoughts of this natural world, then your future will be marked, not by the supernatural blessings of God, but by the sickness, poverty and calamity this world brings.

If, on the other hand, you fill your heart with the Word and the voice of God, if you make living contact with Him each day and feast your heart on His promises and His presence, your future will be one of joy and prosperity, healing and health. Instead of chasing after the blessings of God, you'll find they're chasing you and overtaking you at every turn!

How do you keep your heart in such a state of divine fullness? By doing what we've talked about again and again in this book, by spending time with the Lord every single day and by making that time with Him your number one priority.

Notice I said your *number one* priority. As precious as your family is, it is not the most important thing in your life. (Your family will benefit immensely from this commitment.) Your career is not the most important thing. Spending time with God is the most important thing and once you realize that, you will do whatever you have to do to find that time. You'll wake up earlier in the morning or go to bed later at night. You'll change jobs if necessary. You'll cut things out of your life that steal your time away.

You'll never regret it either, because if you keep that union with the Lord as your number one priority, He will take care of everything else.

"But Gloria," you might say, "that sounds so hard!"

If it were easy, everybody would be doing it. It is difficult in that it takes continual commitment, but it is easy in that it allows the Spirit of God to manifest the blessing of God in every area of your life. It allows God's supernatural power free course. There is no other way. There is no substitute. There's nothing else that will replace time and attention given to the Lord. That's the only thing that will make everything else work. The scripture says:

Be not deceived; God is not mocked: for whatsoever a man soweth, that shall he also reap. For he that soweth to his flesh shall of the flesh reap corruption; but he that soweth to the Spirit shall of the Spirit reap life everlasting. And let us not be weary in well doing: for in due season we shall reap, if we faint not (Galatians 6:7-9).

You might be able to fool yourself into thinking you can prosper by cutting down on your time with God and increasing your time at work, but you can't fool God. You can't avoid His principles. You can't plant one thing in your heart and reap another. Don't be deceived. You can't fill your heart and time and affections with the natural things of this world and have strong faith in the time of trouble.

It doesn't matter if you've been in the ministry 50 years and have the gifts of the Spirit operating through you in mighty ways. If you don't spend time in the Word and fellowshiping with the Spirit of God, spiritually you will come up short. You won't have supernatural power in your life when you need it.

That may sound like bad news to some, but really it's good news! Because the law of sowing and reaping always works, you'll never sow to the Spirit and come up empty-handed. If you sow to the Spirit, you are sure to reap life from the Spirit. You'll reap wisdom and strength and provision. You'll enjoy a continual flow of all that God has and is. You'll be constantly supplied with everything that pertains to life and godliness (2 Peter 1:3).

What Choice Are You Making Today?

Since our future is stored up in our hearts, and every single believer has the ability to keep his own heart full of the Word and the Spirit of God, we all have the same opportunity to be blessed in every way. God is no respecter of persons. God has said to us just as He said to Israel:

I call heaven and earth to record this day against you, that I have set before you life and death, blessing and cursing: therefore choose life, that both thou and thy seed may live (Deuteronomy 30:19).

Your future is not thrust upon you without your consent. You choose it every day—by putting God first place in your life or by putting the natural things of the world first place. You choose it by planting the seeds of God's Word in your heart each day or by entertaining the doubts and fears of the devil.

I said it before and I'll say it again because I want you to remember it: Everything you receive from God starts in your heart. That's where you're born again. That's where the Holy Ghost lives. That's where the Word is deposited. Everything supernatural that you receive comes out of your heart!

Some people assume that because they've spent days or even years studying the Word of God, because they know what it says, they will enjoy a harvest of God's blessing. But remember this, it is the choice you make today—not the choice you made yesterday or last month or last year—that will determine your tomorrow. For yesterday's seed, if not watered today by living contact with God, will be overcome by weeds. The cares of this world, the deceitfulness of riches and the lusts of other things entering in will choke the Word and make it unfruitful (Mark 4:19).

Every day we must obey the instructions in Proverbs 4:

My son, attend to my words; incline thine ear unto my sayings. Let them not depart from thine eyes; keep them in the midst of thine heart. For they are life unto those that find them, and health to all their flesh. Keep thy heart with all diligence; for out of it are the issues of life (verses 20-23).

You deposit the Word in your heart by keeping it in front of your eyes and going into your ears. God has blessed this generation with more ways to do this than any other generation has ever enjoyed. We not only have books, we have cassette tapes. We have videotapes. We have Christian television broadcasts. We have the anointed Word being preached in churches and conventions all over the world.

If we don't keep God's Word in our eyes and ears, it's our own fault!

But even though we have all those avenues available to us, we still have to make up our minds to be diligent. To be diligent means you don't let anything else interfere with what you've determined to do. You can't be diligent and lazy at the same time.

Webster's Dictionary says to be diligent means *to be persevering and careful in work, hard-working and industrious.* It means to do something with careful, steady effort. To successfully keep our hearts and walk in victory in this life, we have to be that way about the time we spend with God and His Word.

If we'll do it, if we'll apply ourselves diligently to keeping our hearts by staying in daily contact with God through the Word and through prayer, His supernatural power will continually flow out of our innermost being. The forces of divine life, forces such as faith, love, joy, patience and the other fruit of the spirit will constantly spring forth from our hearts to empower us and enable us to overcome in every area of life.

Years ago, the Spirit of God gave me an unforgettable illustration of that truth. I was preparing to teach a healing service in the Philippines, and I was meditating on that very scripture in Proverbs 4:23: *"Keep your heart with all vigilance and above all that you guard, for out of it flow the springs of life" (The Amplified Bible).*

As I thought about that verse, I looked out my window and saw the fountain in front of my hotel. The water in it was shooting up in the air with great force.

As I watched it, the Lord drew my attention to the fact that as long as there was an outflow of water from that fountain, no trash could remain in it. Even if it were just barely flowing over the top, it would wash away all debris. If you turned the water up high, the force of it would be so strong that nothing could even get close to the mouth of it.

That's the way our hearts are. As long as we keep an overflow, as long as we have the forces of God coming out of it, Satan's junk will eventually be forced out of our lives and things will be well with us. But we don't have to settle for just a little overflow. We can turn those forces up high. We can have a gusher of God's power, joy, love and wisdom issuing forth from within us.

If we want to, we can be so full of God, so full of the Word and time with Him, that sickness and disease can't even get close to our bodies. We can be flowing so strongly with God's divine life that it becomes as difficult for us to get sick as it once was for us to get healed. If we'll learn to live in constant contact with God, we can experience the divine health that

John Lake described. We can live "day by day and hour by hour in touch with God so that the life of God flows into the body, just as the life of God flows into the mind or flows into the spirit" *(John G. Lake—His Life, His Sermons, His Boldness of Faith,* rev. ed. [Fort Worth: Kenneth Copeland Publications, 1994], pp. 9-10).

You're Building for Eternity

When you think of what's available to us in God, it's amazing not that we find time to spend with Him, but that we find time to do anything else! It would seem with all He has to offer, we would be willing to make any sacrifice to spend time with Him. Look at what we would miss out on. Look at what we would give up: sickness, fear, poverty, sin, unbelief!

But all too often, Christians don't think that way. They're like the people God spoke to in Jeremiah 2:13 saying, *"For my people have committed two evils; they have forsaken me the fountain of living waters, and hewed them out cisterns, broken cisterns, that can hold no water."*

Instead of seeking God, the fountain of prosperity, many believers spend all their time trying to secure high-paying jobs or building big businesses. Instead of partaking of the fountain of healing, they rush to the doctor's office and spend hours there because they are too busy with the natural affairs of life to make daily contact with God.

If you don't spend time every day drinking from the fountain of living waters, I don't care how spiritual you may have been in the past, when Satan comes to put defeat on you, you won't put your foot on his head like you should. Your faith won't be as strong and aggressive as it should be. You'll put up with the devil's garbage. You might pray a little prayer, but it won't have any power because you haven't been making contact with God.

You need to keep partaking of the living waters. You need to maintain an overflow in your heart. You don't always have time to find your Bible in the time of danger or crisis. When you come up against something unexpected, whatever you've been depositing in your heart will come out. You have to stay ready all the time. You don't want to face a life-or-death situation and find yourself without an overflow—and fear and unbelief come out of your mouth instead of faith.

If you do find yourself in that spot, it won't be God's responsibility. It will be your own responsibility. You have a choice. You can feed on Him, the fountain of living waters, or you can forsake Him for the concerns and amusements of this natural world.

Am I saying you should never spend any time on natural things? Of course not. We live in natural bodies and have natural duties we must perform. There are times when it's good to relax and enjoy some recreation. God expects and desires that we enjoy life. He enjoys life and His desire for us is the same. When we put Him first, we live in joy. We get more out of natural life than we ever have before because God manifests Himself in everything we do. In His presence is fullness of joy (Psalm 16:11). Romans 8:6 says to be spiritually minded is life and peace. That's the most enjoyment possible in this life! But always remember this: Every moment you spend on natural things is lost forever. When it's gone...it's gone, and you have nothing lasting to show for it.

The time you spend with God, however, is time spent building for eternity. When it's over, it's not over. Every moment spent with God further opens the door to His wonderful blessings and everlasting rewards.

You are building for eternity right now. The minutes and hours and days of your life are the only blocks you have with which to build. So don't waste them. Use them wisely. Let your spirit be your guide. In other words, listen to your heart. For in the end, it is only the time you give to God that will count.

13

If You Want a Change,
Make a Change

If you're new to the things of God, a beginner just learning about the Word of faith, no doubt you're eager to launch into a lifestyle of living contact with God by spending time each day in prayer and the Word. That's how I was too when I first learned what the Word of God could do.

No one had to urge me to put the Word first place. No one had to tell me to turn off the television and put down the newspaper. I totally lost interest in those things, because Ken and I had our lives in such bad shape that we were desperate for God. We were in trouble. We weren't at the bottom of the barrel. We were under the barrel and it was on top of us.

We knew that the Word of God was the only answer to our desperate situation. So it was easy for us to sell out to it and spend time in the Word and in living contact with God day and night.

You know, desperation sometimes helps. It encourages you to simplify your life. It inspires you to eliminate the unnecessary things and just go for God. But after you've walked with God for a while and things begin to be comfortable, it's easy to lose the desire that you once had for the Word.

That's what happened to me. Once Ken and I paid our debts and began enjoying the blessings of God, I began to let too much of my time be taken up by other things. They weren't sinful things, they were just things I enjoyed doing. Almost without realizing it, my appetite for the things of God began to wane. Instead of hungering more for time with Him than for anything else, I enjoyed other activities and interests more. Those activities would have been fine if I had kept them in the right place, but they occupied too much of my time and attention.

I hardly even noticed it had happened, until one day in 1977 I was attending one of Brother Kenneth Hagin's meetings, and he began to prophesy. (I still keep the final words of that prophecy in my notebook today.) Part of that prophecy said to purpose in your heart that you will not be lazy, that you will not draw back, hold back or sit down, to purpose in your heart that you will rise up, march forward and become on fire.

When I heard that, it dawned on me that I had let myself slip spiritually. I realized I'd become lazy about the things of God. I was still spending time in the Word, but not as much as before, and I wasn't as full of zeal either. (That will always be the case. You can't be spiritually on fire without spending a sufficient amount of time with God.)

The Lord began to deal with me about it. I prayed and determined in my heart that I would change things. In order to simplify my life, I asked the Lord to show me what activities I should eliminate and what I should take on.

He led me to drop certain things out of my life that were stealing my time with God. He also told me to do certain things that would help me get back in the habit of spending time with Him as I should. One specific thing He told me to do was to read one of John G. Lake's sermons* each day. Brother Lake had such a spirit and revelation of dominion that each time I read one of those sermons, it opened up my heart to the power of God in a fresh way.

He also led me to get up an hour earlier in the morning, so I could spend time with Him before I began my day. When I started, it was wintertime. My alarm clock would go off and my flesh would say, *You don't want to get up. It's too dark! It's too cold!* My bed would feel so wonderful and warm that there were a few mornings during the first few weeks that I'd agree with my body and go back to sleep.

I didn't let that stop me though. If I became lazy and went back to sleep, I'd repent. Then I just asked God to help me, and the next morning I'd go at it again! Eventually my body became trained.

Your body can be trained to follow God just like it can be trained to follow the devil. Hebrews 5:14 says that mature believers have their *"senses and mental faculties...trained by practice to discriminate and distinguish between...good and...evil" (The Amplified Bible).* If you practice the things of God, your body will eventually begin to cooperate with you.

For me, getting up earlier was a challenge for a while. But eventually my body learned it wouldn't receive that extra hour of sleep anymore, and it stopped complaining. It became accustomed to getting up at that hour. I also

*John G. Lake's sermons have been compiled into the book *John G. Lake—His Life, His Sermons, His Boldness of Faith,* which is available through Kenneth Copeland Ministries, Fort Worth, Texas 76192-0001.

believe for supernatural rest when I have a short night. It works!

The decision to make time for God every morning has been one of the most important decisions of my life. It made such a difference in my spiritual growth. I'm not the same person I was then. People are always talking about how timid and restrained I used to be. I really was, too, but I got over it!

Become Addicted to Jesus

By implementing the changes God instructed me to make, I created a lifestyle of living contact with God. I became addicted to spending time with Him. Do you know what the word addicted means? It means *to devote, to deliver over, to apply habitually.*

You can create good habits in God the same way you can create poor habits. If you'll habitually apply yourself to making contact with Him daily through prayer and the Word, it will become a way of life to you. You won't even have to think about doing it. It will just come naturally to you.

That's what happened to me. I have developed such a habit of making time with God my first priority that I don't have to get up every day and think, *Well, should I read the Word and pray this morning?* I just do it automatically. It's a way of life for me to spend the first part of my day in prayer now. Even when Ken and I are traveling, even when I have to get up at 4 o'clock in the morning to do it—I do it.

You might think that's extreme. You might think I'm the only one around who is that committed to spending time with the Lord every day, but I'm not. I'm just one of many.

I have one friend in particular who is very diligent about it. No matter how early she has to get up in the morning, no matter what else her schedule may hold, she puts her time in the Word and in prayer first place in her day. That's because many years ago she found herself dying of liver cancer. The doctors had diagnosed it and told her she only had a few months to live.

Medical science couldn't help her, so she turned to God's medicine. She began to spend time reading and meditating on scriptures about healing each and every day. As a result, she is alive and well today with no trace of cancer in her body.

My friend knows she owes her very life to God's Word, so she is still faithful and diligent to partake of those scriptures and fellowship with God first thing every morning. She and her husband are ministers of the gospel and, like Ken and I, they often begin their day very early. But she says, "Even if I have to get up at 3 in the morning, I'll do it."

Certainly such faithfulness requires time and effort. It's not easy. But if believers fully understood the blessings it brings, they too would be willing to do whatever was necessary in order to make their time with God first priority every day.

There are great rewards for that kind of faithfulness! The Bible says, *"The eyes of the Lord run to and fro throughout the whole earth, to show himself strong in the behalf of them whose heart is perfect toward him"* (2 Chronicles 16:9). The word translated *perfect* there doesn't mean without a flaw. It simply means *faithful, loyal, dedicated and devoted.*

God will pass over a million people to find that one who is loyal to Him. He scans the Earth looking for a person who will put Him first and let Him be God in their life.

God wants to help us. He wants to move in our behalf. He wants to meet our every need and work miracles for us. If you were God, wouldn't you do that? Wouldn't you move in the lives of your children? The Bible says if you know how to give good gifts to your children, how much more the Father gives to His children.

Well, we're God's children. We've been born of His Spirit. We look just like God on the inside because He's our Father.

He has us in His heart. He cares about us. He loves each and every one of us as if we were the only child He had. God has a great and wonderful ability to have a family of many millions while treating each member as if they were the only one.

But God can't bless us like He wants to if we won't let Him be God in our lives. He can't pour out His provision upon us if we keep clogging up our heavenly supply line by putting other things before Him. If He is to show Himself strong on our behalf, our hearts will have to be turned wholly toward Him.

Your Desire Follows Your Attention

Maybe today your heart isn't turned wholly toward God. Maybe you're facing the same situation I was facing back in 1977. You've grown busy and lost your appetite for the things of God. You know you ought to be praying more and spending more time in the Word, but you've lost your desire. You just don't want to do it.

If so, you can turn yourself around. You can rekindle your fire for the Lord by making the same kinds of changes I made. Before long, you'll find yourself addicted to God instead of the earthly pursuits that have been so consuming you.

How can I be so sure?

Because God showed me that your desire always follows your attention. Most people think it's the other way around. They think their attention follows their desire, but that's not the case.

One of the greatest practical examples of the fact that desire follows attention is the average golfer. In the springtime when the weather is nice and there is plenty of opportunity to play golf, most avid golfers become very absorbed in their sport. The more they play, the more they want to play. They think about it, read about it, talk about it. They are constantly wanting to play golf!

But when winter comes, they put away their golf clubs. They stop talking about it and thinking about it. They don't mope around all winter because they can't be on the golf course. Why? Because they've turned their attention to other things and their desire for golf has weakened.

I've seen that same principle at work in our conventions. People will come to a Believers' Convention, and when they arrive they will often be completely caught up in natural affairs. They'll be preoccupied, worrying and fussing about some business deal at the office or some problem they left at home.

But after just a day or two of attending the meetings and spending hours on end in the Word of God, they'll completely forget about that business deal and that problem. They'll be so absorbed in the Word that those things won't interest them at all.

It doesn't matter how disinterested you may have grown about the things of God. If you will turn your attention toward Him, your heart will follow.

I know that from experience. I turned my attention to the Word of God, spent time listening to tapes, spent time in prayer until I became so addicted to the things of God that I lost interest in many of the other things that had so engaged me before. For example, I enjoy decorating homes and offices, and I used to spend a great deal of time at it. But as I became more involved in the things of God, I just didn't want to spend much time decorating. Now it's a chore to do that.

What's more, every time I thought about taking up some new project, starting a new hobby or buying something that would require me to spend my time maintaining it, I'd say to myself, *Can I afford this? Can I afford the time it will cost me?* Usually I decided I couldn't. I had come to value the things of God so much and have such great desire for them, I just didn't want to give my time to anything else unless it was absolutely necessary.

A Tithe of Your Time

My resolve to put my time in prayer and the Word first place every day was even further strengthened in 1982 by another prophecy by Brother Kenneth Hagin. In that particular prophecy, the Spirit spoke of wading further out into the realm of the spirit, until it's so deep, you can't possibly touch the bottom. But, the Spirit warned, our flesh will hold us back from that. It's only by renewing our minds that we can move into the realm of the spirit. Brother Hagin went on to say by the Spirit of God that if we'd just give an hour or two out of every 24, our lives would be changed and empowered, *all would be well,* and we would be a mighty force for God.

That prophecy has influenced me and encouraged me tremendously throughout the years, and since I heard it, I have spent at least an hour or two alone with the Lord every day. When I began to do that, there were things in my life and family that I wanted to see changed. There were things in the lives of my children that needed to be improved.

When I heard the prophet say that if I'd spend an hour or two a day with the Lord, things would be well with me, I took God at His word. Today I can give testimony that word was true. It worked. At the writing of this book, everything in my life and the life of my family is good. Things are well with us. My children are healthy, blessed and serving the Lord.

There is no question about it. The time I've spent with God has changed my life. And I can say with certainty that if you'll spend an hour or two a day with Him, it will change your life too.

How could it be otherwise? How could you possibly spend an hour or two daily with the highest authority and the most kind and loving being in the universe without having it affect your life?

You may be facing problems today that seem to have no solutions. You may be caught in impossible circumstances. But I want you to know, God can change those things. If you'll give Him a way into your life by making living contact with Him every day, He'll give you a way out of those impossible circumstances. He'll help you solve those problems. He'll move on your behalf until you can say, "All is well with me!"

If you want a change, make a change. Commit yourself to do whatever it takes to maintain living contact with God, and spend time with Him every day. Determine right now that by the strength and grace of God, if you have to get up earlier in the morning, you will do it. If you have to go to bed later at night, you will do it. If you have to change jobs, you will do it.

Decide that no matter what it takes, you will maintain your communion with God; you will guard your heart above all, for out of it flow the issues of life.

Agree with me now as I pray for you.

Father, thank You for revealing to us the wonderful fact that we can fellowship with You. Thank You for reminding us that we can spend time with You and talk to You. It is such a great blessing to know You'll give us wisdom and reveal to us in every situation what we should do, and then give us help and strength from Your Spirit to carry it through.

I pray for the person who is reading this book right now, Lord. I pray that You will quicken within them a great desire to go on in the things of God, to go on in the walk of faith, to increase spiritually more and more. Give them such a strong desire that it will overcome every laziness, every distraction and every hindrance that has held them back from spending time with You.

In the Name of Jesus, I break the power of the enemy over this precious believer. I release them in Jesus' Name from any spirit of lethargy. I release the power of God right now to rise up within them and come upon them, to endue them with power, Lord, so they can go on and do the things they purpose to do in their heart. Give them the power and the grace to go on and increase and not to draw back or be lazy.

Strengthen them out of the rich treasury of Your glory, Lord, with might in their inner man. Enable them to rise up and be on fire for You, to march and do the things they must do to maintain their time and their union with You at all costs.

We know, Father, that in the end it won't cost us. It will pay us. It will bless us. It might be a little harassment on our flesh for a while, but the Bible says we've been crucified with Christ and that flesh is to be put under subjection. We know we can't do that in our own strength. So we depend on You, fully confident that You will help us, encourage us and enable us to do what we know to do.

Now reveal to those who read these words exactly what they need to do in order to grow and maintain their spiritual walk. Show them what they need to drop out of their lives and what they need to add. Give them spiritual goals they can set to help themselves walk in the spirit. Teach them to maintain a lifestyle of living contact with You.

We give You all the praise, Lord. In Jesus' Name. Amen.

Prayer for Salvation and Baptism in the Holy Spirit

Heavenly Father, I come to You in the Name of Jesus. Your Word says, "Whosoever shall call on the name of the Lord shall be saved" (Acts 2:21). I am calling on You. I pray and ask Jesus to come into my heart and be Lord over my life according to Romans 10:9-10. "If thou shalt confess with thy mouth the Lord Jesus, and shalt believe in thine heart that God hath raised him from the dead, thou shalt be saved. For with the heart man believeth unto righteousness; and with the mouth confession is made unto salvation." I do that now. I confess that Jesus is Lord, and I believe in my heart that God raised Him from the dead.

I am now reborn! I am a Christian—a child of Almighty God! I am saved! You also said in Your Word, "If ye then, being evil, know how to give good gifts unto your children: HOW MUCH MORE shall your heavenly Father give the Holy Spirit to them that ask him?" (Luke 11:13). I'm also asking You to fill me with the Holy Spirit. Holy Spirit, rise up within me as I praise God. I fully expect to speak with other tongues as You give me the utterance (Acts 2:4). In Jesus Name. Amen!

Begin to praise God for filling you with the Holy Spirit. Speak those words and syllables you receive—not in your own language, but the language given to you by the Holy Spirit. You have to use your own voice. God will not force you to speak. Don't be concerned with how it sounds. It is a heavenly language!

Continue with the blessing God has given you and pray in the spirit every day.

Find a good church that boldly preaches God's Word and obeys it. Become a part of a church family who will love and care for you as you love and care for them.

We need to be connected to each other. It increases our strength in God. It's God's plan for us.

Make it a habit to watch the *Believer's Voice of Victory* television broadcast and become a doer of the Word, who is blessed in his doing (James 1:22-25).

About the Author

Gloria Copeland is a noted author and minister of the gospel whose teaching ministry is known throughout the world. Believers worldwide know her through Believers' Conventions, Victory Campaigns, magazine articles, teaching tapes and videos, and the daily and Sunday *Believer's Voice of Victory* television broadcast, which she hosts with her husband, Kenneth Copeland. She is known for "Healing School," which she began teaching and hosting in 1979 at KCM meetings. Gloria delivers the Word of God and the keys to victorious Christian living to millions of people every year.

Gloria has written many books, including *God's Will for You, Walk With God, God's Will Is Prosperity, Hidden Treasures, Living Contact* and *Are You Listening?* She has also co-authored several books with her husband, including *Family Promises, Healing Promises* and the best-selling daily devotionals, *From Faith to Faith* and *Pursuit of His Presence.*

She holds an honorary doctorate from Oral Roberts University. In 1994, Gloria was voted Christian Woman of the Year, an honor conferred on women whose example demonstrates outstanding Christian leadership. Gloria is also the co-founder and vice president of Kenneth Copeland Ministries in Fort Worth, Texas.

Learn more about
Kenneth Copeland Ministries
by visiting our Web site at
www.kcm.org

Materials to Help you Receive Your Healing

by Gloria Copeland

Books

* And Jesus Healed Them All
  God's Prescription for Divine Health
* Harvest of Health
  Words That Heal (gift book with CD enclosed)

Audiotapes

God Is a Good God
God Wants You Well
Healing School

Videotapes

Healing School: God Wants You Well
Know Him as Healer

Books Available From
Kenneth Copeland Ministries

by Kenneth Copeland

* A Ceremony of Marriage
  A Matter of Choice
  Covenant of Blood
  Faith and Patience—The Power Twins
* Freedom From Fear
  Giving and Receiving
  Honor—Walking in Honesty, Truth and Integrity
  How to Conquer Strife
  How to Discipline Your Flesh
  How to Receive Communion
  In Love There Is No Fear
  Know Your Enemy
  Living at the End of Time—A Time of Supernatural Increase
  Love Never Fails
  Managing God's Mutual Funds—Yours and His
  Mercy—The Divine Rescue of the Human Race
  Now Are We in Christ Jesus
  One Nation Under God (gift book with CD enclosed)
* Our Covenant With God
  Partnership, Sharing the Vision—Sharing the Grace
* Prayer—Your Foundation for Success
* Prosperity: The Choice Is Yours
  Rumors of War
* Sensitivity of Heart
* Six Steps to Excellence in Ministry
* Sorrow Not! Winning Over Grief and Sorrow
* The Decision Is Yours
* The Force of Faith
* The Force of Righteousness
  The Image of God in You
* The Laws of Prosperity
* The Mercy of God (Available in Spanish only)
  The Outpouring of the Spirit—The Result of Prayer
* The Power of the Tongue
  The Power to Be Forever Free
* The Winning Attitude
  Turn Your Hurts Into Harvests
  Walking in the Realm of the Miraculous
* Welcome to the Family
* You Are Healed!
  Your Right-Standing With God

by Gloria Copeland

* And Jesus Healed Them All
Are You Listening?
Are You Ready?
Be a Vessel of Honor
Build Your Financial Foundation
Fight On!
Go With the Flow
God's Prescription for Divine Health
God's Success Formula
God's Will for You
God's Will for Your Healing
God's Will Is Prosperity
* God's Will Is the Holy Spirit
* Harvest of Health
Hidden Treasures
Living Contact
Living in Heaven's Blessings Now
* Love—The Secret to Your Success
No Deposit—No Return
Pleasing the Father
Pressing In—It's Worth It All
Shine On!
The Grace That Makes Us Holy
The Power to Live a New Life
The Protection of Angels
The Unbeatable Spirit of Faith
* Walk in the Spirit (Available in Spanish only)
Walk With God
Well Worth the Wait
Words That Heal (gift book with CD enclosed)
Your Promise of Protection—The Power of the 91st Psalm

Books Co-Authored by Kenneth and Gloria Copeland

Family Promises
Healing Promises
Prosperity Promises
Protection Promises

* From Faith to Faith—A Daily Guide to Victory
From Faith to Faith—A Perpetual Calendar

One Word From God Series
One Word From God Can Change Your Destiny

One Word From God Can Change Your Family
One Word From God Can Change Your Finances
One Word From God Can Change Your Formula for Success
One Word From God Can Change Your Health
One Word From God Can Change Your Nation
One Word From God Can Change Your Prayer Life
One Word From God Can Change Your Relationships

Over The Edge—A Youth Devotional
Pursuit of His Presence—A Daily Devotional
Pursuit of His Presence—A Perpetual Calendar

Other Books Published by KCP

The First 30 Years—A Journey of Faith
    The story of the lives of Kenneth and Gloria Copeland.

Real People. Real Needs. Real Victories.
    A book of testimonies to encourage your faith.

John G. Lake—His Life, His Sermons, His Boldness of Faith

The Holiest of All by Andrew Murray

The New Testament in Modern Speech
    by Richard Francis Weymouth

Unchained by Mac Gober

Products Designed for Today's Children and Youth

And Jesus Healed Them All (confession book and CD gift package)
Baby Praise Board Book
Baby Praise Christmas Board Book
Noah's Ark Coloring Book
The Best of *Shout!* Adventure Comics
The *Shout!* Giant Flip Coloring Book
The *Shout!* Joke Book
The *Shout!* Super-Activity Book
Wichita Slim's Campfire Stories

*Commander Kellie and the Superkids*_{SM} Books:

The SWORD Adventure Book
*Commander Kellie and the Superkids*_{SM} Solve-It-Yourself
    Mysteries

World Offices of
Kenneth Copeland Ministries

For more information about KCM and a free
catalog, please write the office nearest you:

Kenneth Copeland Ministries
Fort Worth, Texas 76192-0001

Kenneth Copeland
Locked Bag 2600
Mansfield Delivery Centre
QUEENSLAND 4122
AUSTRALIA

Kenneth Copeland
Post Office Box 15
BATH
BA1 3XN
U.K.

Kenneth Copeland
Private Bag X 909
FONTAINEBLEAU
2032
REPUBLIC OF
SOUTH AFRICA

Kenneth Copeland
Post Office Box 378
Surrey, B.C.
V3T 5B6
CANADA

Kenneth Copeland Ministries
Post Office Box 84
L'VIV 79000
UKRAINE

We're Here for You!

Believer's Voice of Victory Television Broadcast

Join Kenneth and Gloria Copeland and the *Believer's Voice of Victory* broadcasts Monday through Friday and on Sunday each week, and learn how faith in God's Word can take your life from ordinary to extraordinary. This teaching from God's Word is designed to get you where you want to be—*on top!*

You can catch the *Believer's Voice of Victory* broadcast on your local, cable or satellite channels.

*Check your local listings for times and stations in your area.

Believer's Voice of Victory Magazine

Enjoy inspired teaching and encouragement from Kenneth and Gloria Copeland and guest ministers each month in the *Believer's Voice of Victory* magazine. Also included are real-life testimonies of God's miraculous power and divine intervention in the lives of people just like you!

It's more than just a magazine—it's a ministry.

Shout! The Voice of Victory for Kids

Shout! ...The dynamic magazine just for kids is a Bible-charged, action-packed, bimonthly magazine available FREE to kids everywhere! Featuring Wichita Slim and *Commander Kellie and the Superkids*$_{SM}$, *Shout!* is filled with colorful adventure comics, challenging games and puzzles, exciting short stories, solve-it-yourself mysteries and much more!!

Stand up, sign up and get ready to *Shout!*

To receive a FREE subscription to *Believer's Voice of Victory,* or to give a child you know a FREE subscription to *Shout!,* write to:

Kenneth Copeland Ministries
Fort Worth, Texas 76192-0001

Or call: 1-800-600-7395

(7 a.m.-5 p.m. CT)

Or visit our Web site at: **www.kcm.org**

If you are writing from outside the U.S., please contact the KCM office nearest you. Addresses for all Kenneth Copeland Ministries offices are listed on the previous page.